The Secrets
of
Aleister Crowley

Amado Crowley

© Amado Crowley 1991

All rights reserved.

No part of this publication may be reproduced, stored in a retrieval system, or transmitted in any form or by any means, electronic, mechanical, photocopying, recording or otherwise, without prior permission of the copyright holder.

Published by Diamond Books, 29 High Street, Great Bookham, Leatherhead.

First edition 1991.

ISBN 0-9517528-0-4

Printed in Great Britain by BPCC Wheatons Ltd, Exeter

Contents

1. **PHRA**
   A Bald Outline – Causes Celebres – The 'Irritati' – A Double Life

2. **SEBEK**
   Head above the Ramparts – Secret Tests – Why publish now? – Quiddities – Good Red Herring

3. **AMENHOTEP**
   The Rebel – The Clique – Blanco or Blacking – The Fiend

4. **TAURET**
   The Actor – Crow's Feet – Theorem – Casanova

5. **HATHOR**
   The Chalice – Boyfriend – Boulogne – Sultry Magnificence – The Cuckoo

6. **IHI**
   A Small Murder – The Summons – First Meeting – The Toy – My Name

7. **HOR-NUBTI**
   Neighbourliness – Hey Presto! – Folkestone Meet – The Dovecot

8. **SHU**
   Romney Marshes – Tadpoles – Cliff Path – Vertigo

9. **BENNU**
   Monotheism – Paganism – The Devil – Former Friends

10. **NEBTHET**
    Master Race – Ancient Powers – The Great Beast – Calumny

11. ANPU
    Trinity Church – Ghosts – The Dead – The Black Mass – Rosemary's Baby

12. SEKHMET
    Spoils of War – A Hero's Death – Mum's the Word – Sea Shells

13. ANHUR
    Leaflets – Foxy Lady – Canterbury – Human Sacrifices

14. ATUM
    Singing Gongs – Automatic Writing – Our Joint Work – Pink Religion

15. SESHESTA
    The Queen of Sheba – Rastafarians – Caesar – Aiwass – The Sacred Book – A Missing Page

16. HOR-MERTI
    MI5 – Pressures – Official Secrets – Telepathy – Underworld

17. UPUHAUT
    The Admiral – Assault on Asgard – Darling of the Gods – Two Germans

18. MENTHU
    Supper at Arundel – Provocations – A Bishop Translated – Ashdown – The Bird Flies

19. MAAT
    A Nation's Gratitude – Silent Witnesses – Odic Forces – Double Cross – Crimson to Purple

20. BASTET
    Witch Queens – Night Hags – Magic Ointment – Antique Origins – Why does it Exist?

21. MIN
    Gerald Gardner – The Commission – Crowley Gate –
    The Secret Door

22. RENPET
    Are you Ready? – The Mark – The Sand Pit – The Hand

23. TA-DHENET
    What an Initiate is – Apprentices – The Stone Circle –
    The Strange Boat – The Mystic Words – The Climax

24. DJEHUTI
    A Summing Up – Three Flaws – The Ungodly? –
    Quick Change – Drugs

25. OURSIR
    An Overstated Case – The Importance of His Magick –
    An Awkward Customer – Master of Evil?

26. KHENSU
    Crowley's Appearance – Gurdjieff – Curious Parallels –
    Unknown Teachings

1
PHRA

The sovereign lord of the sky and Creator

A Bald Outline

Edward Alexander Crowley was born on 12th October, 1875 at the small town of Leamington Spa. His father, also called Edward, was head of a brewing company, and both parents were members of the repressive Christian sect known as the Plymouth Brethren. Throughout his childhood, there were nightly bible readings.

When he was only eleven, Crowley's father died, and his mother moved to London, placing her son under the wardship of her brother, T. B. Bishop, who despatched the boy to a school run by the Plymouth Brethren in Cambridge. The mental and psychological cruelty he suffered under that regime gave him a lifelong detestation of Christians. At one point in his youth, he was in such a sad condition that a doctor warned that he might die before he reached majority. He was packed off on a tour of Britain with various hand-picked gaolers.

It comes as no surprise then, that when Crowley made his first ever visit to a theatre, he looked at the audience in amazement. "Aren't all these people afraid of being found out?" he asked his companion in great sincerity.

His formal education was at Malvern and Tonbridge schools, and at Trinity College Cambridge. During these years he wrote some very promising poetry and became a well-known mountaineer. He and several friends formed one of the first parties to attempt to climb Chogo-Ri, the second highest mountain in the world.

He also became a member of The Hermetic Order of the Golden Dawn in 1898, at the age of twenty-three. Toying with the idea of entering diplomatic service, he went to St. Petersburg in 1897 where, on one of his many outings, he went to visit the Khlysti, or Men of God. He met, and had a relationship with, a young married monk called Gregori Rasputin, who was then 26 years old.

He climbed through the various grades of the Golden Dawn quite rapidly and declared himself Magus in 1915. Crowley also changed his name from Edward Alexander to Aleister. This was the only permanent change but at other times, he put on and shed whatever other names or titles appealed to him, e.g. Prince Chioa Khan, Count Svaroff and Lord Boleskine, to name but three.

As a reaction against the repressions of childhood, Crowley taught that magical sexuality played a supreme role in the revelation of truth. He had learned this from Rasputin who, you remember, became intimate with the Tsar and Tsarina of Russia.

In 1912 he was visited by Theodor Reuss, a high-ranking German Freemason who worked for his country's intelligence service. As regards his doctrines on sexuality, Reuss accused Crowley of revealing some of the closely guarded secrets of the Ordo Templi Orientis. Somehow or other, instead of quarrelling, the two men got on very well indeed and Reuss installed Crowley as the head of the O.T.O. in England — which may well have been the real purpose of his visit all along.

At various times in his life, Crowley picked up and appointed several "scarlet women", who played the symbolic role of "whore of Babylon" to his "Great Beast of the Apocalypse". But in the U.S.A. — where else? — he met the woman who was more suited than anyone to the role. She was Leah Hirsig. When the First World War finished, the two of them founded the Abbey of Thelema at Cefalu in Sicily. This was intended to be a kind of seat or university of occultism, but rumours and alleged scandals led to his expulsion by the Italian government.

Causes Celebres

He was expelled from various countries at various times for doing things that were otherwise quite common in the streets of their own capitals! One can say that the man's life appears to have been a succession of legal causes celebres. But most of these were to do with libel, sexual permissiveness and copyright. Certain newspapers found it good for their circulation to mount campaigns against Crowley. He made excellent copy, and the British public read every journalistic detail of his 'steaming' private life. He studied those newspapers himself in order to penetrate the role he was expected to play. But it was the magazine John Bull which dubbed him "The King of Depravity", "A Human Beast" and "The Man We'd Like to Hang". But the headline which stuck, and the most famous title ever hung round his neck, was: "The Wickedest Man in the World".

That, very briefly, is Aleister Crowley's life. Or rather, it is the rag-bag out of which most authors create their colourful collage of opinions. People regard him as a bit of a circus ring-master with more than a touch of the sexual roué. They also know that he was very probably the founder of modern occultism. With this crude material, you can create whatever kind of case you wish. If you don't like him, and many people loathed him, there'd be no trouble making him out as a monster. In actual fact, he did nothing very bad at all. If he committed the same acts today, we'd assume he was a member of parliament.

As I will explain, Crowley was the victim of a conspiracy whose main aim was to make sure that his teachings would never be taken seriously. So they zoomed-in on the horseplay and, as we all know, the conspiracy succeeded... until now, anyway! One of my aims in writing this book is not to whitewash his name but simply to tell some of the other truths about him, i.e. those truths that have been repressed. I would like him to be judged against all the facts.

The 'Irritati'

My book will get some backs up. I'd love to be wrong, but what a fool I'd be to imagine it could be otherwise. Let's be realistic: talking about Aleister Crowley is like taking nitro-glycerine to a "bring-a-bottle" party! The name, by itself, has a most extraordinary effect on people. I have found that the Great British public, or those who know about him, are either *for* him or *agin* him, and *extremely so* in whichever case. I've learned to live with that. I have come to expect it. Aleister Crowley is remembered for all the wrong reasons, and that is why I shall probably tread on a great many toes.

I went to a birthday party once. I felt quite safe, so just for once I didn't bother with an incognito. If you're in cancer research, everyone wants you to feel their lumps. If you're a psychologist, they want to talk about their dreams. With me, of course, the whole world and his son want to broach some aspect of magick. Could I cast horoscopes, they asked? Had the spirits left any message for Molly? And would I care to make a prediction about the winner of next Wednesday's big race? For some reason I never quite understood, someone wanted to know if I could put a curse on their vicar! It was quite refreshing to come across a gauche American girl. She chatted away so breezily I wondered if she'd mistaken me for a casting director from Hollywood. In any case, I wasn't equal to her liberal use of slang. She'd had it with Voodoo, she said. It freaked her out. Californian witchcraft had been big, but that freaked her out too in the end. It seemed that in the very short space of her youth, she had worked her way steadily through every available cult and sect in America — including even the Sioux Indian sweat chambers! All of them had freaked her out.

Aleister Crowley though, now he was real hairy! I found this quite intriguing, considering how the vast majority of people remember him as being totally bald. "Would it freak you out," I asked with sarcasm, "to know that I'm Aleister Crowley's son?"

She stared straight at me aghast. I could feel myself undergoing some type of ghastly mutation under her very eyes. "Aw, aw," she croaked for about ten seconds and then "Awww shi-i-it!". She vomited copiously and explosively. Quite tall she was, with a very bad aim! I should not have tried to be witty, I guess.

Another reason why I won't be very welcome is that the occult scene teems with experts already. Most of them pride themselves on knowing all there is to know about Crowley. I can see how they will react when they learn that they do not. They are not going to be best pleased.

Then there is family. I am not by any means the only child he had, either in or out of wedlock. Most of the others discreetly changed their names a long time ago. Still, they may not welcome some of the revelations I make. The infamy and the disgust are still there, even if people are not quite sure of their reasons. When the New Towns Commission first lit upon Crawley, in Sussex, as a likely place to develop, they actually questioned the wisdom of leaving it with that name. It is in the minutes!

Not that I can afford to laugh, because I too have kept my head down. Of course, certain gentlemen will call me an impostor on the grounds that Crowley never told them about me — and he would have done so. They are very sure of themselves. In fact Crowley knew which ones were likely to crow too loudly and guessed what they'd do with his secret. They betrayed all his other confidences, didn't they?

Whatever others may say, they cannot be sure. They are just surmising, whereas I possess proof. Not that it matters. It is what I say about him that counts. Let us just take one example: why are so many of them still attacking Crowley half a century after his death? That would be a nice little subject to ponder over, eh?

When you've worked it out, you'll understand why I tread so carefully.

A Double Life

I have done my best to write an objective account. But he was my father and though I knew him very well, I was young, and our relationship lasted only seven years. Anyway, that is more than most others can say, and the relationship we had was very intimate.

The text is mine then, but the ideas, opinions, theories and attitudes are all very much his. Whether or not I agree with his doctrine or advocate it to others is a private matter and it would be out of place to talk about it here. Aleister Crowley was a rash person. He acted on the spur of the moment and was often wrong. He could be very thoughtful too, and some of his considered opinions may offend certain groups today. Please: I have no wish to offend you. I would prefer not to become an occult Salman Rushdie. I rely on my memory but where I am unsure of my facts, I do say so. I have tried to do my duty by him. I hope he would approve.

Somebody will ask: "Why didn't you announce yourself before this? Why didn't you let your presence be known?" How convenient if I could say that this is how he wanted it, that he sent me some secret, death-bed instructions. But that would be lying. The truth is, I was scared! I was in my teens when he died. I knew even then that if you're the son of Aleister Crowley, you do not boast about it. I was doing National Service, hoping to go straight to university after. When I saw how my comrades drooled over the stories, the day that he died, I decided I just hadn't got it in me to be a freak at a side-show.

Also, he had given me things that I was supposed to guard. I am not using that as an excuse, but that job was more easily done if certain people never found out where I was. Oh yes, this probably sounds paranoid, the flawed logic of a cracked brain. Take my word for it: it was just plain old cowardice. I could live without any fuss, so I kept my head low.

2
SEBEK

The god with the head of a crocodile who came from the dark waters to bring order to a world in chaos

Head above the Ramparts

At the age of forty, I became less craven. No, I didn't grow out of it but, having found a sinew somewhere I stiffened it. Some twenty years ago, for instance, I wrote an open letter to a weekly occult publication[1], and they printed it in an edited version:

> "*A LETTER FROM 777*
> Aleister Crowley, notorious magician and self-styled Great Beast 666, died in 1947. There has been a remarkable revival of interest in him in the last few years and, some months ago, an undated letter, signed 'Amado Crowley 777' was sent to *Man, Myth and Magic* in a plain envelope with a London postmark. The author says that his interest in Crowley stems from the fact that he is Crowley's illegitimate son. We have no way of checking the authenticity of this statement but we feel that the following extract from the letter may be of interest to readers.
> It is claimed by '777' that Crowley fathered him in order to have an heir who would carry on his work and to this end he gave him careful and secret instructions... etc, etc."

You can hardly call that hiding my light under a bushel. But between my father's death and middle-age, I did keep a low profile. There was my career, you see — my everyday work. I

---
1. BPC Publishing Ltd, *Man, Myth and Magic* No. 81, London 1971.

was a psychologist, a university tutor, and a chief examiner for a national award, all of which clashed badly with my other role as an occult Master. There was quite a conflict, I promise you. Above all, I was conscious of not doing my duty, of not meeting the charge that Crowley had put on me. In addition, the 'call' itself was repeated more and more strongly, and I felt embarrassed... if not ashamed. Up to then, I had been a very reluctant magician!

When at length I did put on the fallen mantle I continued to be the soul of tact, and not without reason. As I will explain later, I held many secrets and there were, and still are, people who'd like to get their hands on them. I'm not just speaking of young weirdos, or over-zealous devotees of Crowley or of Magick. I mean groups, departments and organizations with a world-wide face. You will have to take my word for it: this is why I did not blab my head off. As regards my career, I don't think anyone cottoned on. I got the reputation for being slightly unsociable, reserved, and not someone who would join a rugby team or drop in for cocktails. In that respect I was probably quite unpopular. But that was the price I had to pay.

Secret Tests
It is a term used nowadays by closet homosexuals, but once I 'came out', a lot of people suddenly wanted to meet me. Some came as individuals, or so they said, while others claimed to be emissaries from occult orders and secret societies. There were also a couple of my father's old chums, a couple of cranks, and one delightful old boy who wanted to track down a crate or two of 'Crowley's Ales' if they were still available.

Way back in 1969, I had a desultory relationship with some people from the cast and orchestra of the musical show called 'Hair'. In 1970, a pop-group called 'Stone the Crows' and their lead-singer, Maggie Bell, crossed my path. They dropped me like a hot-brick after the lead-guitarist was electrocuted by a faulty contact in the equipment. I have also met Jimmy Page of 'Led Zeppelin' — he owned Boleskine House, incidentally, and wondered whether he might install me as caretaker and tourist guide.

I was summoned by Kenneth Anger to an 'abbey' in the home counties. The flags were out and the grounds fluttered with occult pennants. The place was not his, he assured me. He'd just borrowed it from a friend. Out of courtesy to that friend, I won't be more precise. Nevertheless, Mr Anger spent the day carefully putting me through one test after another. An encrusted cope lay casually tossed over a bannister. I knew full to well whom it had belonged, but I had no intention of demeaning myself. There were other special objects innocently strewn here and there. I was a bit too big for baby-games and this procedure put me in mind of the way they choose the next Dalai Lama. I did not play ball, and he decided I was a write-off. Evidently, it doesn't count if you see what their little game is.

On another occasion, I met a charming German-speaking gentleman at an exclusive hotel not far from Sloane Square. It was so exclusive that you wouldn't even guess that it was a hotel and you were scrutinized before you were allowed in. Perhaps it was a private club or residential premises owned by an exclusive organization. My host did his best to put me at my ease. When he quizzed me for three hours before inviting me to take a coffee, I realized he was Swiss. According to Aleister, Swiss hospitality means offering you company but you pay yourself for anything that passes your lips. It's what made Switzerland the great nation that it is today.

But this particular Swiss made a false assumption. He thought by acting inscrutably I would learn nothing at all about him. But it was clear that he'd been sent by the Crowleyite Temple at Zurich. I didn't show that I'd seen through him. I just told him some of my father's less virulent views on the people of the Helvetic Confederation. I failed his tests quite easily.

To be honest, I've failed every single test that they have ever put me through! There have been American ones, French ones and even, would you believe, Japanese ones! Over the last thirty years, I've sat patiently through something like a hundred similar interviews. I am so used to them, I've had so much practice, that common sense would tell any ordinary person that if I wanted to pass them, I would know how to do it! But it never crosses their minds. Each thinks he's the first, you see, and all of them presume that Aleister taught me nothing! I know quite well the answers they are looking for. The trouble is, they don't know the question that I am waiting to be asked!

It's sad, when you think about it. All these groups tramping along the path my father's finger indicated before it fell in death.

Yet here I am, carrying out his wishes, and teaching the ones who are humble enough to see my light instead of being dazzled by their own. Crowley said it would be so. He said they'd be blind to the truth. "A chain of events will alert you," he warned. "Give each of them a chance to open the seal. The key will be a particular question." No one has ever asked it. At least, not *yet* anyway. These worthy people have been so intent on measuring the herald, they forgot to ask why he'd come.

Why publish now?
Unlike my father, I don't enjoy the limelight. That is why I have never tried to publish a book about occultism before. I am more interested in teaching people, and I belong to the school of thought which thinks that this is best done in a face-to-face situation.

"Then why write this book now?" I can almost hear you ask. Well there is a story behind that, and quite an interesting one too.

I no longer live in England. I come back regularly to visit groups and students, and to visit my mother, now in her spry eighties. I also stock up with good books in English. It's less expensive that way, and dodges the problem of reading dear old Clive Barker in Albanian. What I do is go into Watkins in Cecil Court, not to ask for credit like my father, but to see what's new and interesting. I am either over-optimistic or too undiscriminating. I go back laden with books by the armful, but many get hurled on the fire or given to charity sales.

Obviously, it takes time to get through them because I buy enough to keep me going until my next visit to England. That's why it took some time to get round to 'The Games of the Gods' by Nigel Pennick[2]. How stunned I was to find a sizeable chunk of material that I had written myself some twenty years previously. No, nothing as ambitious as a book, but articles which had been stencilled and circulated by students. What made me cross was that Mr. Pennick called it *authentic Saxon material*, when I had told my students it was all my own work. Someone somewhere might begin to think I was a liar.

My first impulse was to turn Mr. Pennick into a bright green frog. But I thought better of it and wrote a letter of complaint to

---

2. Pennick N. *Games of the Gods*, Rider, 1988 pp 40-41.

the publishers. To cut a long story short, Mr. Pennick apologised and promised to acknowledge me as the source of the material in any future reprint. The odd thing was though, the editor invited me to lunch whenever it would be convenient.

They wanted me to write about Aleister Crowley. No, they were not in any position to actually commission a book, but it was my filial duty to tell the world my side of Aleister's story. They made it sound so noble I would have felt churlish to refuse. They gave me lunch in a Greek restaurant where the waitress was a newly-arrived cousin from Cyprus. She spoke no English but had learned the menu parrot-fashion. When we asked about the dish of the day, she said she wasn't like that and gave us all moussaka!

The editor, an utterly charming and quite delightful lady, was still working hard to overcome my dwindling resistance. To whet my appetite, she improvised madly, plucking a whole series of possible titles out of thin air. Some were full of zest, some were maudlin, and one or two quite upset me. I got her drift, though. I cottoned on to her line of thought. The book I was to write should be full of revelations and secrets. "How about: "My Dad Died of Apocalypsie'?" I asked. Luckily, she did have a great sense of humour, and was honest enough to blush.

"From a commercial point of view," she went on unabashed, "it does make sense. What a sensation it would be if you describe the other face of Crowley, the one that nobody else has seen. Paint a new portrait and from a different angle." I had cold feet, I must admit. The moussaka wasn't helping me much. But something spurred me on and told me to think again. I had retired, after all, so I need scarcely worry about the effect on my career. I was a full-time teacher of occultism. "So what have you got to lose?" my conscience insisted. In the end I said "Yes". It was as simple as that. The company undertook never to reveal my address or my pseudonym. Just to be sure, I never gave it to them. Business was done through middle-men or via post boxes belonging to other people.

All very awkward but... you can never be too careful.

Quiddities

I sent the company an outline for the whole book, together with some sample text. They replied with a few suggestions like "cut down the bits about yourself", and "concentrate on Crowley".

In due course I submitted the revised material which was satisfactory. But by the time I sent a complete first draft, the publishers had been taken over by an even bigger organization. Not only was the whole policy changing but the editor herself was moving on. Alas, she informed me rather briefly, they would not be interested in the book I had written.

She was under some pressure herself, at the time, but I did feel it was a bit thick to whisk me on my way at quite the speed she did. A year of my life wasted! All that work for nothing! I was quite devastated. The project had now taken hold of me. I had the feeling that my father too was urging me on. The very next day, there was Aleister Crowley's photograph splashed across a page of The Sunday Times along with the heading: His Beastly Beatitudes. It turned out to be a review by Snoo Wilson of yet another version of my father's life[3]. This was a double coincidence because I knew Snoo Wilson. When the Royal Shakespeare Company produced his play 'The Beast' at their other theatre, near St. Pancras, I had been invited to help the actor, Richard Pascoe, with his characterization.

"Hello," I thought. "If that's not a bell being rung, I am a Dutchman!" So I telephoned the publisher of that book, had a meeting, and was told it was ninety per cent certain they would have it on their lists. They didn't though. Their list was full and they felt my manuscript needed to be printed quickly, probably because of the rules to do with the release of government documents.

We photocopied the manuscript and sent it to a score of publishers. Their replies were either plain rejections, or very significant, depending on your point of view. A good few of them telephoned to say how interested they were. Then they would come back again, after a board meeting, to say they had changed their minds. Yes, of course, it could just be a bad book. Or it could even be a good book which lacked commercial appeal. But what does one make of these two extracts from genuine replies:

"... it would not do my company's reputation any good to publish a book that put Crowley in a favourable light."
and

---

3. Symonds J. *The King of the Shadow World*, Duckworth 1989.

"... Strangely, I doubt if you'll find anyone in England to print it."

I am not a professional writer. I never intended to rival Catherine Cookson. But I do wonder a teeny weeny bit whether someone hasn't been leading me up the garden path — just to see how much I know. As you probably all realise, the Freemasons are quite well represented in certain parts of London. Not the slum areas, of course.

Anyway, that is how this book was written.

Good Red Herrings

This isn't just one more list of scandals and sleazy innuendoes. It's not a book about magic either, not as such. The reader with a sharp eye and a bit of insight stands to pick up several hints and indicators. But my main purpose has been to talk about Aleister Crowley and the true facts of his life. Yes, inevitably, I will throw some light on his ideas because just to talk about the real man helps one to understand the things he actually said. So you may breathe easy. This isn't going to be one of those popular books on "how crystals can cure haemorrhoids" or "using acupuncture to pass your driving test". I once went into one of those tiny magic supermarkets where they sell anything and everything. "Curses for all purposes", sort of thing. The man behind the counter had the well-studied air of one who knows more than any normal person should. If you'd asked for a Hand of Glory, he would have offered them fresh or stuffed!

Business was booming. The place was full of young folk: girls in shawls, boys in ethnic shirts, and everyone in a haze of heavy Indian incense. I tried to talk with him. My age showed I was not from the police, but he assumed I was deaf. "Truth is like pot, grandad! You get the quality you pay for!" Everyone in the shop giggled. Oh yes, a real occult community where loving thy neighbour meant helping him carry his wallet. It was the voice of a true salesman, but not a teacher of truth! The snag is that young folk can't always tell the difference. They are inspired by impulse and moved by excitement.

Fair play though. Beggars and hustlers have always been there, eager to cash-in on men's fears, faith and dreams. It is the same with every creed. Look at the rival offerings to draw the tourist: the Buddha's tooth — the Wailing Wall — the footprint of the

Prophet — the bones of martyrs — the Turin shroud — and naturally: Stonehenge!

It's a sorry thing to say, but magic always has been for hire. Even Aleister Crowley would peddle charms, pills, potions and spells — but only when he was broke, which is as good as saying: most of the time! He could even lay on his hands, if you promised not to jump. Dear, dear! The shepherds are fleecing the sheep of Xanadu. Why are they so blind? If they are pilgrims, why do they behave like a carnival crowd? They'll waste their youth looking for light, and all they'll have left in later years is trinkets that once throbbed with vibes.

Nothing fills a cinema like an X-certificate. In the occult industry, the nearest equivalent is Aleister Crowley. His name can almost make cheques sign themselves. In other words, he's what the cockney fly-boys call "a nice little winner". But I'm not one to begrudge a chap his living. I have nothing against the former taxi-driver who went through Hyde Park and came out at Atlantis. I don't condemn the spirit-medium who takes down dictation from the ghost of Nostradamus. But I draw the line at plastic replicas of Excalibur and fairy Tarot cards from Wales. There is a limit. There is a boundary. I'm sorry to turn solemn but after a certain point, the fast buck verges on evil.

"Fine talk", one might say, "and him setting up shop as Aleister Crowley Junior". Come on! Do grow up. What sort of ninny would *pretend* to be that man's son? If I wanted to be an impostor, I'd have chosen a model that was easier to live with. Sheer common sense says *don't pick Aleister Crowley!* Let me tell you, it has been a very mixed blessing and so far I haven't made a penny! So if I'm a fraud, I'm also a failure.

I am not ashamed to be his son but I don't feel particularly proud either. I'd be very unhappy to be changed into the Duke of York. I'd have even more to complain about if I were changed into his wife. But, if you see what I mean, I have never *not* been Aleister Crowley's son so it feels... just ordinary. It's as familiar to me as seeing my own face in the mirror. You have not heard of me? But that's the point! If I've not exploited my name before, why the hell would I start in my sixties?

In daily life I use my mother's married name. I disguise my real identity and my whereabouts. As you read the book, you will understand why I make it hard to find me. Just for now, accept my apology. My story is a true one. The only things I have doctored are minor details that might help the wrong people to find me.

3
AMENHOTEP

A sage and an initiate of the holy books. No man better understood the mysteries of the rites

The Rebel

When people think of Aleister Crowley, they remember those farcical photographs. There is one of him in Arab gear, another where he poses as a fat Chinese god, and a few where he strikes dramatic, theatrical poses.

When I last saw him, he was older, thinner, and lacked many of the good things of life. He was a sad, rather pathetic figure who reminded me of a neon tube which had started flickering.

"I hope your friends will serve you better than mine did me," he once said. "At all events, you shouldn't count on any aid from my little lot."

As usual, he was quite right. They have ignored me totally or they have treated me with the kind of cold contempt that Joan Crawford reserved for young actresses she didn't much like. Gerald Yorke was the only one who showed me any kindness. He offered me the old man's pocket chess-set as a keepsake but I said no. As for the others, they let me know how cheerfully they would have throttled me. Except they were too old and didn't want to risk pitting their power against mine.

Oh, he knew what he was talking about, did old Aleister Crowley. So he should have: he was a magician! It is the very first thing one must say about him — that and the fact that he had more impact on occultism than anyone else before or since. What's more, his influence is still growing. It gets bigger and bigger, all the time. It rolls through the calumnies like a snowball through skittles.

As the years pass, new generations stumble on Crowley afresh. They are not such hypocrites as their parents or grandparents. Far from being shocked at the so-called scandals, they admire the rebel in him. So they read his books more hungrily, they admire him more sincerely, and the old boy's prestige keeps on climbing. In his own day, he was radical, too extreme; but the world has moved on now and, lo and behold, popular feelings have caught up with him. He was against racism. He believed in the equality of women. He saw nothing wrong in homosexuality.

He scorned class privilege and regretted his own bourgeois origins. It proved a big obstacle between him and working people because he was unable to get through to them. Occultism was the pursuit of "gentlemen", a bit like exploring Africa: you needed money and you had to have free time. In word and deed, in public and private, he mocked the cant and humbug of the establishment. Which was very unwise of him. The establishment turned against him at a very early age.

But all that *and magick too!* No wonder he is such an intriguing character. With all the money his work brings in, he'd get the Queen's Award for Industry today. He'd probably have a franchise system with 'Magick Centres' in between Laura Ashley and the Body Shop.

It is hard to believe he's been dead for forty odd years!

The Clique
Aleister Crowley is dead though. Or at least, they cremated him in Brighton on 5th December, 1947. So the guru is gone, his mouth is closed, and he has not spoken outside the seance room for nigh on fifty years. It doesn't stop his name cropping up however. I tried to calculate just how many books have been written about him but stopped when I passed the two hundred figure. And that doesn't include his own reprints, lengthy quotations and references. Hardly a year goes by without another biography appearing — often by the same author! One could say certain folk have dedicated their life to him or rather, they earn their livelihood by him. Like Shakespeare, they have turned him into a lucrative business. He would have found that funny. He never made much money for himself but the hangers-on do quite nicely. "Leeches", he would have called them, if not something much more phallic.

In Crowley's hey-day, society was very much like a well-kept sideboard and everyone knew where he belonged. The people lodged in each drawer were marked by their own speech, accent, style of dress and rules of behaviour. Railway trains had first, second and third class carriages which were intended for the elite, the worthy, and the workers respectively. Men were either owners or traders and the rabble were just toilers. The only way to climb at all was via night-school classes. Every town in the smokey North had its Mechanics Institute where they taught "useful trades". Needless to say, there were no classes in Greek, Latin or any of the purely academic subjects! There was no call! The study of occultism wasn't all that common, but it was more respectable than today. High-class people did it, you see. But Crowley's brand of occultism put most people off, and fascinated just a few. The ones who were drawn to his side were special or, if you prefer, odd. It's much the same today, in that respect. The ones who seek are the ones whose needs the current system cannot meet. So yes, occultists do tend to be eccentrics, weirdos or social misfits. There was never any great, popular movement surrounding Crowley. It wasn't like the Boy Scouts or the Salvation Army. His flock was small. People floated in and floated out again. In no way could they be seen as a typical "slice of society".

It is hard to guess what he would have called the scholars and experts who 'reveal' new meanings, 're-paint' his own words, or 're-hash' his rituals. I don't know if they are sincere when they pretend to be servants of the Law of Thelema. I am not sure what kind of satisfaction they get from forming new groups and netting in new members. But they never knew Aleister Crowley, so how the hell do they know 'where he was at'?

They have no licence and no authority. They get away with it for the very simple reason that he is dead. He is in no position to sue. A dead person has no civil rights, as such. That may be why they think they are beyond his reach now. I wouldn't be so sure. He was not a very forgiving man. He bore grudges for years. If I were them, I'd sleep in my track-suit and keep my third eye open.

Blanco or Blacking?
A dead leader is more convenient than a live one, whether in religion or politics. He has said all that he is ever going to say. The doctrine is complete. The way is open for any one to learn it all by heart and set up shop as a worthy successor. Peter and Paul did it, I believe, and to avoid a split, Peter got the job of

figurehead, and Paul dictated the party-line. But a Master who still has breath in his lungs could upset the apple cart. He could change his mind, for example, and tear up his old ideas in favour of newer and better ones — which would make the pretenders look real fools.

It is not unknown for 'a chosen few' to betray or even kill their holy leader, especially if he's going ga-ga or starting to have regrets. Sudden 'turns for the worse' and 'unexpected heart attacks' seem to be an occupational hazard, as presidents, popes and even popstars could testify.

Besides this, death does tend to hallow someone's memory. The day before, he's being torn to pieces by his critics; the day after, you can't see the body for wreaths. Howling for his blood one minute, tearing their hair out in grief the next. You can see this most often with regard to the stars of the silver screen. They have been fading away in an Old Folk's Home and no one has given them a thought. The day a death is announced, the tributes flow in, the cinema pays homage, and the television grabs gratefully at this chance to make a new programme. And that is where you will see all the other ephemeral butterflies of fickle fame: in the queue, shuffling toward the coffin, waiting their turn to shed some tears for the cameras.

It is worse still in France. Whenever they run short of money and are desperate for something to transmit to the viewers, up they come with another retrospective. "Five years already", they proclaim before trotting out all the old material. "Ten years already". When that gets too much, they will have a programme where everyone votes which was the best film, best actor etc during the last fifty years! To make things even more parochial, the French believe that all culture ends at the Paris ring-road.

When a great person dies, what is it that determines which way the pendulum will swing? Who decides whether this was someone who merits a nook in the Pantheon, or whether his corpse should be chucked into an anonymous pit?

I suppose it helps if you have become "a legend in your own lifetime", as the cliché has it. On the other hand, if you were mocked and despised, they might regret it later — Harold MacMillan, Danton, King Charles II. That's not what happened with Crowley though. "I shall be a thousand times more popular when I am dead," he said. "A point I have in common with Jesus

Christ! But then, he did have a twin brother to help the mythology along.[1]"

The Fiend

As I have said already: they have chucked everything they could at Aleister Crowley, yet his name ranks highest in the history of modern occultism. This is not what they intended, surely? It wasn't just enemies or rivals who attacked him; old friends too tried to get in on the act. Nobody has a good word to say about him. I find that very strange. Of course, one must not waste time on deciphering a code that isn't there! All the same, during his life they stopped him from being taken seriously, and since his death they have gone on attacking his memory. Bad luck they were so incompetent.

It's so obvious, I'm surprised no one has complained. They go for Aleister's jugular with all the fury they can muster. But they do not attack his occult theory. Thereby hangs a tale! Kings, politicians and military men have done things that make Crowley as innocent as a new-born babe. But they had title, position and PR men. Crowley relied on himself. The worst that can be said is the man was a fool and as naive as a sitting duck. He knew about evil, but did not understand about people's wickedness. There was no Saatchi & Saatchi in those days. He made a mess of his own publicity.

He hadn't always been famous, you see. He began as a nobody but pushed himself to the centre of the occult stage and hogged it. He nettled the wrong people. He upset the barons of Fleet Street. He got under the skin of the Freemasons. He also made royalty uncomfortable. Altogether, their combined resentment became a kind of holy war. This book is not going to please them. It will be interesting to see where they will concentrate their attack. Of course there are occult groups about whom he never said an ill word. They have never spoken against him either.

But poor old Crowley was such an innocent that he even crowed about the bad publicity he got. The more they blackened his name, the more he was pleased. True, he was a visionary — more attuned to '*that world there*' than '*this world here*'. It can't

---

1. Baigent M, Leight R, Lincoln H. *The Messianic Legacy*. Jonathan Cape 1986.

be the whole explanation, I agree, but he had no time for social niceties and he didn't give a fig for protocol. A square peg in a round hole, you might say — but scarcely a criminal for all that. What outraged society more, I think, was the way he brazenly flaunted his disapproval. He was vain, he loved dressing up, and he could cock a snook better than anyone else around. To put it in a nut-shell, he destroyed people's dignity!

This was a grave fault. When it rose to the surface, he lost all insight and it required immense patience and generosity to be his friend. He was not an unsavoury person, just difficult to know! Despite all these problems, he never abandoned his quest for truth. According to his own lights, everything else was trivial compared to that one goal. It wasn't too hard to link his name with black magic. But "the most evil man who ever lived"? or "the spawn of Satan"? No! Nevertheless, the innuendo has done its job. He didn't see it coming. He minimized its importance. He never imagined that such absurd labels would stick.

"Pshaw!" he scoffed. "Sticks and stones!"

Obviously, he was not a good judge of things!

4
TAURET

The goddess of maternity and suckling, often represented as a hippopotamus

The Actor
No one disputes that Aleister Crowley was a true magus. But he was tactless with it, very pompous, and had an in-born gift for getting up people's noses. He was also rather buoyant, larger than life and very much "over the top". There was an actor *manqué* in him with the ranting genius of another Donald Wolfit, and the same tendency to ham. He probably knew people in the theatre, though I doubt if this is where he got his ideas for "the magick voice" which he emphasized so much.

But what of the face behind the make-up, the man behind the stage character? Did no one ever realize that *Aleister Crowley* would be a good title for a melodrama? It would be useful to know how much of the posturing spilled over into his private life. Had he read 'Phantom of the Opera'? Did he let anyone see underneath his own mask? He was a human being, a man, but... he was, 'on stage', a large part of the time. For that one reason alone, there is a lot about Crowley which has stayed unknown.

Most of the stuff we hear today is based on third-hand hearsay, most of which was spiteful. The people who put their thoughts in writing had less talent, yet coveted the principal role. Praise, where you can find it, is grudging. Hints are sprinkled among the attacks that far worse things have been left unsaid. But oughtn't we to have expected this? It isn't every day an understudy writes about the star, and it isn't too surprising that he gives us warts and all.

One other thing: Aleister Crowley had a certain air, or he exuded a certain force. Hard to put one's finger on it but when you met him, you felt obliged to adopt a stance. You couldn't ignore him.

You weren't allowed to think things over and form your opinion later. He had the knack of thrusting himself onto your attention. Perhaps it was a theatre skill, like not turning your back, and projecting your voice to the gallery. It was partly charisma too. The world is drawn to such men. Not just friends or family, everyone is pulled by a magnetism they feel.

Persons like these are turned into idols, or targets. It's just as easy to do either. But one has to react. One can't simply live with it and carry on whistling. But then, you see, just as with a total eclipse of the sun, people's reactions to such a phenomenon are shaped as much by their inner fears as their external perceptions. Some folk were irritated by him. Others fell in love with him. A minority felt as if their mind (some mind!) was under attack. Only a mere handful asked him to be their guide. But no one felt impartial. Nobody walked away unmoved.

Crow's Feet
It comes to all of us, sooner or later: a wrinkle, the weakening eyesight and the first streak of grey. One ages. One mellows. One begins to dwell more and more in the past, thinking of absent friends. In 1928, Crowley's thoughts turned more and more towards eternity. He was quite capable of stirring up the occasional scandal still, but a new bee was buzzing in his bonnet. The top notch magician of the entire century had decided he wanted a child!

He'd had a brace or two already, of course, and was not quite sure of the exact number. A few he had heard about in the natural way of things. But there were others who were never announced. The women never asked for help with money. They wouldn't have got it anyway. If they'd been close enough to get pregnant, then they knew he was usually broke. They never rebuked him either. He hadn't set out to seduce them. If anything, the boot was on the other foot! Women couldn't resist him and set their sights on him. They just walked up and offered their all. One accosted him on the very steps of a law-court!

"The spirits have ordered me to bear your baby," she said. Crowley leafed quickly through his diary. "Would Wednesday at two-thirty suit?".

Now I ask you: what judge is going to condemn a chap for being appealingly virile?

That sort of thing apart, he had never wanted a baby before. "Trifles caused by trifling", is how I heard him call them. "I may be chosen to plough the sods, but blame nature for the thistles!"

Not that he wished his children the slightest harm. Quite simply, he didn't want to know. It was somebody else's concern. Their life was their own to live as they wished. It's as well for them, for all of us, that he took this stance. He would have been an incompetent father and a bad provider. His time was taken up with things of cosmic proportions. Who dare ask that he stop fighting evil just to change nappies? It was a common attitude in those days too. Let's be fair about it, his own parents were not exactly an ideal model.

By the time he reached his mid-fifties, his views were beginning to change. They do, you know. A sea-change comes over them. You've been everywhere and you've done everything, then suddenly one day you realize there is unknown territory on the horizon. That brings you up short. He was nothing like old, of course, but the clouds he knew were lined with purple. He had a terror of turning senile. I don't think there was any special reason for him to worry. But there it was: a horror of becoming decrepit and dependent.

"It is my idea of hell," he told me, "to be a shrunken mute, at the mercy of some cocky, gymnastic young man in a white coat." He spat this out, with his usual touch of acid humour, but he was also very sincere. "If ever I have a stroke, if ever I end up in that state... I count on you." He would take my hand and squeeze it like an orange. "You will push my wheel-chair up a mountain and leave me there... with a cup of hemlock and a straw!"

This one phobia apart, he was never morbid. He was not the kind of man to wallow in black moods or depression. He seemed never to be overwhelmed by dark thoughts, and though he had to deal with things that made my hair stand on end — he tackled them in a workmanlike manner and whistled. He wasn't even afraid of the idea of old age or of dying. He just didn't want to end, as he'd begun, like a baby. Until that day came, he worked hard not to waste time.

This was the real reason he decided he needed a son. The family business needed a successor. The child must help realise certain plans that had simmered at the back of his mind for years. He'd put it off, and kept on putting it off, the way one does with bills or subscribing to a pension scheme. Now he wasn't too sure of himself. It might already be too late. It was probably the most critical decision of his entire life, and a great many other things depended on it. And yet he was reluctant to have a go. He was nervous in case he blew it.

Time, he now realised, was not on his side.

Theorem

It would be a boy, of course. A girl was out of the question! Not that he was sexist, but he knew what was expected of him. The gods wanted a son!

The mother, the vessel for his seed, would have to be special too. One way or another, she must possess those qualities which would add certain touches to the child's character. For the boy to match his plans, he must pick the mother with care. Just to make it all the more complicated, the exact moment of the conception would have to be prearranged. This could prove to be the trickiest part of the whole scheme. Women are not best kept on the simmer if you have a stop-watch in your hand, and ejaculations in the mid-fifties are not at your beck and call!

He had already selected the location for this act of magick. The latitude and longitude and even the polarity of the bed! He was nothing if not thorough. Evidently, this was not going to be just another anonymous bastard. This was going to be a bespoke, Crowley special, crafted by supernatural means and hallowed to the cause.

But there was one other reason for being nifty. Old friends in Germany were advising him that a Second World War was inevitable and the storm clouds were already gathering. Using his own psychic gifts, Crowley foresaw that millions would die, that atomic weapons would be invented, and that the seeds of desolation would be spread around the globe. When you carry the title 'The Great Beast 666', this kind of news brings a whiff of the apocalypse with it. This could be the day of doom approaching.

All the more urgent then, to conceive the chalice 777. He would be the new teacher for the Aeon of Horus. He would be the Aquarius from whom the healing waters would flow. Everything must happen well before the explosion.

To add still more urgency, the spirits warned him that the lack of a fitting disciple could be a calamity. Aleister Crowley knew the exact date when he would die. He also knew that his son would need to have achieved at least a certain age before then so that he would have grown in size. He needed a frame that was strong enough because, when all is said and done, a Master's mantle is heavy.

Time was of the essence. Things had to happen quickly. But who was the woman? Where was she living? In what sort of life-style should his boy be raised?

Casanova

He set about it with the same zeal that Henry VIII had when he tried to divorce Catherine of Aragon. It felt even more important than 'the King's Business', as he started looking in spring, 1929. At this same time, he was also looking for someone to publish his "auto-hagiography" and with Crowley, it is not impossible that the two things were connected.

His calculations specified someone very unusual: she must carry both the blood of Gipsies and the blood of nobility! She must be as near twenty-one as possible and born under the sign of Sagittarius. To meet the prescription to the last detail, she must be from the North of England and be living in the Woollen Ring, of all places. I have no idea why these conditions applied. Perhaps he didn't really understand them himself. On the face of it, this seems a very tall order — like looking for a needle in a haystack. But when you think about it again, you begin to see how easy the gods were making it. Quite an extraordinary shopping-list, to be sure; but on the other hand, there could only be one person like her. Finding her would not be the problem at all — but getting at her, that would be a different kettle of fish.

Despite all that has been written about him, Crowley never saw himself as God's gift to women. Just look at him, for heaven's sake. He lisped, he was asthmatic, he took drugs, he was fond of alcohol, he was fifty-four, he was penniless and... he was as bald as an egg! This was no legendary lover. Kojak possibly, Yul Brynner certainly, but Aleister Crowley — never! To put it as kindly as we can, this was no Adonis!

But he had a way with him. He had a certain knack. My father knew how to wheedle, coax, cajole and persuade. He could do it effortlessly. Men as well as women! He could wrap them round his little finger and turn them to his will. Part of it was innate charm, and part of it was magick. This was a man who could throw enchantment over others.

I saw him do it. I knew when he switched it on. He would just look at them while he was speaking and their brains would buzz like telephone wires on New Year's day. He did not use this gift indiscriminately or irresponsibly. I think there was a price to pay in terms of inner energy. Nor did he only use it in order to get close to others: I have seen his presence quieten people's fears, allay suffering, and bring peace to the dying. People believed in him. By simply being there, he could vanquish their doubt. Perhaps I'm getting fanciful; how would I tell? But it seemed to me that people just melted like snowmen in the sun.

He was not mad or crazy. Whatever the press tried to imply, this was a man in full control of his faculties. He never saw himself as any kind of saviour or redeemer and, in having a baby, it was not his intention "to sire the next Messiah"! As a matter of fact, although he despised Christianity in general, and certain sects in particular, he respected the real Jesus and saw him as another Master. But as far as his own child was concerned, he wanted no stars, no shepherds, and no unwelcome kings on camels. It goes without saying that a virgin birth played no part in his plans. All would be natural, with a teeny touch of the supernatural.

Master Therion aimed for two goals in this campaign. First, he needed a colossal amount of power. Second, he must nudge it in a certain direction. It must all be achieved without draining the source and without putting his life at risk. This is why he chose one of his own hansels to the Order of the Golden Dawn: the Eleventh degree Maithuna rituals. This is often cited as proof of Crowley's alleged bi-sexuality. In the past, such a thing was worth pursuing since it caused such revulsion it could really injure a person's reputation. Nowadays it would not provoke such horror and, in any case, his personal tastes are irrelevant. Still, this is where some folk get hot under the collar, and you know what they can be like: once they get emotional, they stop thinking sensibly.

The Maithuna Process, Eleventh Degree, of the Golden Dawn, does not seek pleasure but power.

Once the operation was launched, Crowley drove himself like a man consumed by a dream. It had now dawned on him that even if Merlin was not immortal, his flame could survive.

5
HATHOR

The great celestial cow who is goddess of joy and love

The Chalice
Her name was Stella Taylor. She was just twenty-two and worked in a Yorkshire mill. Naturally, in those days, the West Riding of Yorkshire meant "wool", and all the towns I mention depended on the textile industry. One place made worsted suiting, a second concentrated on carpets, and a third on blankets. The smallest village could have its speciality — spindles, shuttles, bobbins or dyes. After the Second World War though, the industry shrank. It is now about one tenth of its former size and people's life-style has changed.

Stella's mother had been a gipsy. Her family moved from one fair to another, but always made sure they arrived at the race meetings at Thirsk, York, Wetherby and Doncaster. Among the many famous races, the 'St. Leger's' at Doncaster has always been the most popular in a Northerner's heart. That and the Grand National are more popular than Christmas or Easter as markers in the year. Those who can, flock to Doncaster. Those who can't put a bob or two on their favourite. The gipsies are there because they once traded horses. Now they set up their stalls for tipping the winner or telling the future. Every one of them claims to be descended from Gipsy Rose Lee — they know she is famous you see, but they don't realize what for.

Stella's mother met her man there. She read his palm and he told her everything he could about himself. He was the illegitimate son of a titled mine-owner. He was a collier himself and had a bad temper, a strict sense of right and wrong, and he loved her. They married and had five children, only two of whom died in infancy, and that was good going in those days. The monotony and fatigue of the mines, the frustration of life in a hovel, soon drove him to extremes of unpredictable anger. One day, when she couldn't stand it any more, she just upped and left him. She arrived by bus in Leeds, with her little brood and two suitcases, and received a lukewarm welcome from a younger sister. She did laundry, scrubbed steps and anything else to earn enough money. As soon as she could, she left her sister's grudging charity and moved into rented rooms at Dewsbury. That is where Stella grew up.

Boy-Friend

It was hard being the eldest. She was the first to leave school, the first to go to work, and the first to find a boy-friend. In fact there was no shortage of them because Stella was a beautiful young woman. She knew how to turn cheap clothes into things that she had seen in the films. Bits of fur added here, old buttons cut off and replaced by something unusual. As for hats — her hats were the talk of the weaving-shed!

Courting was the most difficult bit. Home was just one room up and one room down. The shared lavatory was a hundred yards away at the corner of the street. There wasn't a lot one could say or do, even if her mother went to bed early to leave the couple alone, she would cough regularly to let them know she wasn't asleep, and as it got late she would call down "Don't forget you have to be up at six!" The cinema, the Princess Picture Palace, was the only place for privacy and there it was tricky. They were far stricter in the North. When cinemas were first erected, chapel committees saw them as "occasions for evil" and put pressure on town councils to impose restrictions. The lights were not to be dimmed too far. Usherettes with flash-lights must patrol the aisles four times an hour and tap any canoodlers on the shoulder. Actually to be expelled from a cinema was so ruinous, girls would leave home. This wasn't the only risk. Snotty-nosed kids would giggle and make filthy comments. Old folk would snort and mutter that it should be stopped. Even more irritating was the fact that Stella would get engrossed in the films. He was working himself up to a lather while she was willing her heroine to escape from the railwayline. Her boy-friend, Len, got quite sulky.

In those days the railways were privately owned, with the major lines split between four or five companies. Len worked for one of these, The London Midland and Scottish, as it was called, or the L.M.S. Because of this connection, he was allowed to buy his own railway tickets at a cheaper rate and use several other perks. That was how he hit on the idea of taking her away for a naughty weekend to France. One imagines quite well the sort of thing he had in mind, but Stella had visions of exquisite perfumes, haute couture, and a kiss from Charles Boyer.

The whole street knew about it. They got all puffed up and pink at the very thought of the scandal. It wasn't that they were setting off, and them not married. Oh no. Easy enough to say you had separate rooms, and no one was going to argue about it. The source of their outrage was the fact they were going to France! That is what put the fat in the fire! Why France, they demanded? Why not Blackpool or Filey, like any other decent couple? France was flouting custom. France was flying in the face of nature. In brief, France was taking things too far!

There was something very cheeky about it too, as if the usual lies weren't good enough for her! That young madam had her nose in the air, her and her flair with clothes. It was just as if she were setting out deliberately to make other folk jealous.

Worst of all, married women had told them a thing or two about France. About how their men had changed once they'd been there. How, after Armistice Day, they came back smiling when they shouldn't have! So everybody knew that France was not a bit like England.

Boulogne

She went pale as soon as the train stopped. The moment she clapped eyes on the boat, she felt her stomach heave. "I can't go," she said, turning pale. "I'm turning back!". Her chap, Len Standish, tried taking her mind off it. "I can speak a bit of French," he said.

"How do I ask for a bucket?"

He laughed and said it was a good joke. But she wasn't joking. She'd seen Charlie Chaplin's film about immigrants on their way to New York. Being the great comic he was, he had pretended to be sick. She didn't have to pretend: she threw up in the cinema. So finding herself floating on the surface of the sea, she couldn't think of anything else, no matter how hard she tried. The precise second that the engines started, she ordered Len to leave her. He could go to the bar if he wanted. She was going below decks to find somewhere to die. She spoke just like Lilian Gish, and in sepia too.

She clutched her little handbag in one hand, and walked through the benches as if they were battling through a violent storm. They hadn't left the dock yet, but if she felt sick, then sick she was going to be. And not just any old sick, either. This was going to be spectacular. She was going to be sick on a grand scale. She was quite right too. In no time at all she went from grey to green, less like an English rose — more like a spray of dead Irish shamrock. It was there that Aleister Crowley found her, on the ferry to Boulogne. Until recently, passengers who felt ill were told to lean over the railing on the leeward side. But the time lost looking for the few who fell led to the introduction of enamel bowls. If the crossing looked rough, the bowls were spread out on the benches. It was the first thing you saw when you came aboard — the sad line-up of these cracked, alarming bowls.

Men would buy a bottle of duty-free brandy. Women would go for eau-de-cologne and a box of extra-strong mints. The smell of that incredible mixture — brandy, mints and vomit — is what most people associate with their first visit to the continent.

The great magician stared at her for a while. She lay like Cleopatra after the asp had gone, with one arm thrown across her eyes to shield them from the terrible glare. He had no second thoughts. The fates had not played a joke on him. She was very beautiful.

His eyes gleamed calmly, as if they were ship's lanterns lulling the sea. He smiled ever so gently, and the pitching and rolling grew less and less. Stella was aware of odd things happening inside herself as the entire upheaval began to bate. She felt a hand stroke her brow. His first touch. Their first contact. She heard him mutter strange words, and thought he must be the ship's doctor. She couldn't recall whether she had taken some medicine or if he had given her an injection. At all events, his treatment was working very well: it did seem to help. Perhaps he stilled the fluids of her inner ear. Maybe he just jammed the shrieks from the vagus nerve. Magic always prefers the most economic means. As Aleister once said: "No point holding a Jubilee Mass just to cure a bunion."

She wasn't worred how he did it, she felt better and that's all that mattered. The blood came back to her skin, the nausea lifted, and she gave his hand a squeeze.

Sultry Magnificence
I don't know how she saw him. So soon after her ordeal, he might have seemed handsome. Or did she react immediately to his

strange magnetism? His face was as radiant as the sun after a storm. She emerged from a hellish experience into his smiling arms, and she could have sworn there was music. Something tingled in her arms. A hidden flame sped along her nerves. It was like a close-up in a Garbo film, and the air pulsated with power.

"Are you feeling better?" he asked in his kindest voice. "Much, much better," she signed tranquilly. "With all thanks to you."

She felt as cosy as Sunday, the day when workers could lie abed and dream their dreams. Sunday was the quietest day of the week. There was nobody in the streets before eleven o'clock, except perhaps a kid or two going to fetch the papers. They'd take a drink at the pub just before dinner, a nap after, and then the walk in the park till tea-time. Oh she loved Sundays.

So she lay back now, reclining like Jean Harlow. She let herself bask in the love-light that she saw in his eyes. He was a gentleman, no doubt about that, and after the mould of Eric von Stroheim. It was as if she and he had stepped out of the screen and her fantasy had become real.

"It is our destiny to meet," he told her. "I have looked for you everywhere." It was all quite true, of course, but she added her own moonlight and violins. "Now that I have found you, you must let me come for you." Oh yes, he was playing up to her. He told me years later that he knew all about her great love of the cinema.

Stella wanted so much for all of it be true that, of course, she made it true. She had her own kind of magic and it was quite potent. This was not a street-corner lout. This was a gentleman. That much was obvious from his clothes and the way he spoke. He didn't talk common — but he didn't talk posh neither. He was just... nice... and so friendly. This was the kind of man who would feel at ease sitting on red velvet chairs and snapping his fingers at waiters. He would know how to order champagne or whistle for a horse-drawn cab. He had sat in gondolas, ridden on the Orient Express, and smiled from a box at the opera. There was no need to rely on any strategy. Stella was willing to eat from his hand. She impressed him too. As far as appearance goes, she was a woman who made the best of herself. But she had charm and real spirit too. When he looked at her, he had the power to see her as the sum totality of all she had been in her previous lives. He was more than content and he thanked the gods for having helped him choose aright.

I don't know if he had any grounds for saying it, but he told her she had once been a great actress. Certainly she never had any difficulty in putting on a show or doing a turn. It ought to be easy then, he explained carefully, to go on being ill even after they had landed.

"You mustn't overdo it, naturally. But you can send your young man to have a look round the town rather than both of you waste time in your room." He kissed her hand and gave a conspiratorial wink.

"But you shall not waste your time, of course. I shall see to that. I will send a car for you. Shall we say, nine o'clock?"

"Do you know where we are staying?" she asked naively. "I will just tell the chauffeur to follow the light," he replied.

The Cuckoo
Len Standish had a couple of drinks and, just when he was getting bored, he bumped into another Englishman. The chap was extremely friendly and they hit it off like nobody's business. He had had some luck at the casino and was going to paint the town red. He was taking Len with him. Stranger still, he started Len off with a modest stake, and very soon he too was raking in the chips. All in all, he won four hundred pounds in the space of five hours. That seemed like a small fortune in those days.

As for Stella, it all came about like a fantasy, a dream, a film with John Gilbert. Someone came for her and conducted her a short journey through the night. There was a chateau, a party with champagne, and she let herself flow with its bubbly charms. There was laughter, music, dancing and then... a new kind of ecstasy. Not an innocent, not without experience, this was the first time it lived up to expectations and really felt like making love. She realised it would never be the same again. When she re-awoke in the modest hotel in Boulogne, she wondered whether it had all been real or just a fleeting dream. But there was no time to ponder over that. She must focus her mind on making it up to Len and salvage his naughty weekend.

Just one year before all this, Crowley had been ordered to leave France, along with Israel Regardie and a current ladyfriend. Much had been made of the story and another small scandal created. Oddly, though, Regardie and the woman had been sent packing at once, but Aleister Crowley was given a few weeks' grace on the grounds of ill-health. No one has ever commented on this, but in fact it was all arranged by persons close to the government. While his friends waited for him in Brussels, he was holding talks with men from the French secret service.

The outcome was that despite the "official" ban, Aleister could come and go as he pleased, as long as he was discreet and let them know in advance.

Len was stunned, a few weeks later, when Stella told him she was pregnant. He was still in a state of confusion, two months later, when they got married quietly at the town's Registry Office. In one way, he felt he was very lucky. But in another way, he couldn't work out how or when he had been responsible. But there was the evidence, visibly growing before his very eyes and he knew she'd never been out with another bloke.

They moved into a small rented house of their own, and when the boy was born, 26th January, 1930, he just muttered that it was grand. For the first fortnight, their little home was thronged with people all coming to have a look. Each brought the customary gift, though not all of them were new: knitted bootees, a shawl, a dozen nappies and a rattle. That sort of thing. Many tongues wagged when the railway van stopped and the driver came in with a parcel. It was a toy rabbit. An enormous toy rabbit. As big as a four-year old child and dressed in a suit with a colourful waistcoat.

It was from his grandad, Stella explained. He was a coalminer down in Kent. They would call it Wilfred after him. "His grandad's name is George," Stella's mother hissed. "I should know. I was married to him!"

The aunt and uncle, both still in their teens, crowded round the cot with glee. "He looks more like you than Len," they said. All of Len's family agreed.

6
IHI

The sistrum player, son of Horus and Hathor

A Small Murder
Aleister Crowley longed to build a band of kindred souls, or a kind of inner brotherhood. He wanted to use a process called "soul-bonding" to raise a forgotten type of collective power. The way I grasped it, it was not unlike nuclear fusion! The Golden Dawn could count on fifty to sixty loyal members. Its influence derived not from any significant occult achievement but from the clout those few people had in the world outside. But none of them stopped it falling into ruin. That is why Crowley arranged for a watchful eye to be kept on Stella and her baby.

The men who read the gas-meter were too polite. The woman from the sanitation department was too quick with giving a grant. Above all, an old widow-woman two doors away took a sudden interest in everything that went on. Stella tried her best to keep up appearances, but as Len grew more jealous, suspicious and violent, the sentinels grew more vigilant. In one outburst, the enraged father hanged and killed the boy's dog. In another, he shoved the lad's fingers into an electric socket. It was feared he was losing control. They pinned their hopes on the second baby. She should calm him down. But at one month she was stricken by pneumonia and within a few weeks she was dead. In a moment of anguish, Stella accused Len of having deliberately killed the child. He just replied that it wasn't his anyway. That made her more fearful than ever for the safety of the boy. At the funeral tea, the child said something to make his father crack.

"Me and her was playing," he announced, "and she told me what you did."

"Lying little bastard," scream Len, knocking the child off his chair and across the room. In the shocked silence, everyone stared at him mutely. "For God's sake," he appealed, "he's only four years old!"

"You took her blankets off when me and Mam was asleep. You opened the window next to the cot."

Len's face went as white as chalk. He gaped at the boy, his nose pinched. "You never played with her," he charged. "She never played with anybody. She has been too poorly since the day she was born."

They treated pneumonia with a steam tent, for the breathing, and kaolin poultices for the infection. We believed these poultices 'sucked up the badness', which is why they were carefully burned.

The boy trembled. "She gave me the poultices you took off."

"The nurse burnt them!" croaked Len.

"And the flames were the colour of peacocks."

The man sent some glasses flying. "When did he ever see a peacock?" he howled. "He doesn't even know what it is!" "It's got a hundred eyes," the child sobbed. "They blink when there's rain or pain. It cried when you told me she was dead."

Stella left him. She took the child and two suitcases and walked out of the house. The widow-woman met her and urged her to see a solicitor in case Len made trouble. The one she advised had a familiar face, but he whisked them through the formalities and obtained a legal separation. Stella could keep the child. Len would pay maintenance until he was sixteen. He didn't. She never insisted. We lived with grandma in a cramped slum at Brighouse.

The Summons

After that, life was quiet, poor but passably content, and nothing much happened until round about the month of November in 1936. A letter came from Crowley asking her politely to bring the boy to see him. The only kind of mail that families like ours ever got was either seaside postcards or Christmas greetings. A letter was exceptional. Telegrams were objects of terror, often kept on the mantlepiece and not opened for days. He enclosed a pair of return tickets from Bradford, and told them to arrive on the 25th of January, which was the eve of the lad's seventh birthday. Although he had never been on a train before, the novelty soon palled and the journey was long and wearisome. At Crewe, a nice man came on board just to give them a small cardboard box containing two packed lunches. When at length they arrived at

Euston, another man carried their luggage and took them to Victoria in a taxi. The driver was amused at their eager gawping from the window. "Look," he said, "that's where the new king lives." The boy saw only an enormous statue on the traffic island and wondered if the royal children played in the road.

Victoria station was even busier than the other one, and the halls were awash with people dashing to the boat-train. "This way for France" said a signpost on an iron stand. Stella's eyes went misty for a moment. Nearly eight years. The attentive guide whose eyes missed not a thing, let a very faint smile cross his lips. Then, as if proving how heedful he was, he led them to the public toilets and escorted the boy inside. It all went as smoothly as a Swiss watch: trains were on time, their seats were reserved, and neither of them felt any travel sickness, as Stella had feared. Even the connection and the short trip across London, had been free of trouble. It was almost as if their way was charmed. She had done her best to ready the boy's mind for the looming encounter. It was not an easy thing to explain. But while she squirmed and felt very awkward, the lad listened with his eyes wide, and asked no questions at all.

"You copied me when you heard me calling your grandma 'mother' and you dodged any problems by calling me Mam." She grinned and tried to win a smile from him. But the little boy was agog, hanging on her words. "Well, it's a bit like that with your dad," she went on. "Except he's not your real dad. You called him that because, well, I was married to him. You'll meet your real father today but, because we're not married, we are keeping it secret."

There had been no cause for worry. The boy didn't care twopence and there was no need for anyone to explain. He was wrapped up in the sense of mystery that shrouded it all and his mind was already weaving magic stories around the bald facts. The closer the train carried them to his presence, the higher the tension rose, not in fear or distress, but more in youthful suspense. When they got to his house, afternoon tea was waiting, and then they had soothing hot baths to relax them after the day-long journey. It was some two hours later when they were finally ushered in to his study. Despite the heavy curtains, the noise of cars came through the large windows.

"That is the trouble of a house near the capital," said someone with a slight speech defect. "People working there don't like staying there, so the home counties have this ebb and flow of damnable traffic every morning and night. In between it's cows, carts and the rattle of milk-churns! You would think it either a madhouse or a zoo!"

This then was the very first meeting between father and son.

First Meeting
He greeted Stella with kindness but there was no warmth in it, not that she was offended. His attention was all for the boy who met his scrutiny with no sign of shrinking at all. In a visible attempt to start things rolling, the man asked him if he liked this part of the country.

"Is it any easier to get to France?" asked the child.

'That is a very odd answer," snapped the other.

"Oh, that was not my answer," observed the boy, "that was just my beginning."

A sharp glance flashed between the two adults, and Stella shook her head in response to the unspoken question that shone in Crowley's eye.

"Do you like France?" the piping treble voice asked next. This time the man's eyes held an impish twinkle. "I have some very fond memories," he replied, and Stella blushed. "They are going to hurt it, you know. They will be coming soon, screaming to set it on fire," said the boy.

The man was silent, unmoving, and there was nothing to read in his face. His eyes rested on the boy quite calmly.

Stella was nervous in case he thought that the boy was sick. "He often comes out with strange things like that," she tried to explain lamely. "He told his grandma she would die in St. Luke's. He told a neighbour about a fire at the mill. He even said the king would leave his mother." She gave a shrug, half apology, half because she didn't know what else to say.

"And is he right?" The man looked at her firmly. "The things he says: do they come true?"

For quite a long time, she did not answer as if reluctant to commit herself. "As often as not," she mumbled at length. "As often as not?" he echoed. "As often as not?" he repeated once more. His eyes opened wide and he bent towards her like a grandad coaxing a child. "As often as not?" he said one last time.

The woman was almost crying. She was out of her depth. These were things she could not deal with. They made her very uneasy. Whenever she could, she tried not to think about them, afraid of what they might signify. At the time of writing, my mother is still alive, a spry eighty-two years old. She has never once talked about these things during the last fifty years, apart from occasional remarks like "His dad was like that," or "it's in his blood". She has great faith in my "second sight" as she calls it, and never stops embarrassing me by discussing many examples of it, even with mere acquaintances. Now Crowley was drilling into her brain and she knew it was time for the truth. As often as not? he had asked. She nodded like someone giving in.

"Always," she replied.

The Toy

He did not kill the fatted calf and there was no great revelry. Why should there be? I wasn't the Prodigal Son who'd been lost and found again. He knew where I was: a piece of left luggage to be reclaimed later. I would have liked to quiz him about that. I found it very odd and was deeply curious — as well as feeling just a wee bit resentful. As a matter of fact I refused to warm to him for quite some time and he knew why, all right.

No, he was not what you would call a devoted father. He had made me and had done his best to protect me. But love? It didn't enter into it. Several years later, he did once try to put me in the picture. Even then he expressed no regret because, as far as he was concerned, the whole venture had been one hell of a success. "I do not feel much sympathy," he told me. "It may help you if you try to understand that love, for me, is something of a mystery for me. That is something I hope your mother will teach you. My mother did not teach me."

He was my father in a technical sense but not in the way he related to me. We were more like teacher and pupil than father and son. It felt much more like a formal or professional relationship than a truly personal one, as you'd expect. I did get fond of him though and, as we grew more familiar, I believe he felt some real affection for me. It is so difficult to tell you how it felt. A disciple on special terms with his master is as near as I can get. He did that job very well indeed. There he felt at ease. He could command unknown forces and control secret powers, but a large slice of the emotional spectrum seemed to be beyond him. To be perfectly fair to his memory and as neutral as it is possible to be, the word "home" held no meaning for him. At first, he probably saw me as a model, or something he had planned and built by hand. I was a prize item in the collection, to be sure, but kept at a distance. I was his. I belonged to him. He treated me very much as an author might deal with a chapter he was checking — and not as something that had a separate existence. I always had the sensation of being put in good order for publication. I was not part of his family. He never had one.

He explained his plans, and they agreed that I would stay with my mother. He said it was prudent, she said it was essential for a young lad. I saw him several times a year up to the age of fourteen and usually spent my summer holidays with him. — As far as I know, my mother never discussed these matters with my grandmother. We were still living in her house at the time but she asked no questions and raised no objections. When she and I were alone, all she ever asked me was: "Did they feed you well?" — I was quite content with all of this. As far as I can remember, I think I savoured the little hints of secrecy and the notion of a special mission. It put me in mind of the films I liked at the Saturday matinees. I quite fancied myself as a captured prince, a kidnapped heir, a baby suckled by apes or, best of all, Mickey Rooney — Mickey Rooney was a great favourite with children at the time. He made his debut in 1928, playing Puck in 'A Midsummer Night's Dream'. We liked him most in a series of 'Andy Hardy' films in which he was teamed with a girl called Judy Garland.

My Name
The boy asked what he should call him. Crowley hummed and hawed and said that 'Master' might be best all things considered.

"Oh," laughed the child, "but that's what they call me. They always write it on my birthday cards: Master Andrew Standish."

The man laughed too at the absurdity and the charm of this tiny child and tried to explain things patiently. "In one instance," he said, "Master is a polite way of addressing young boys. In another, it is the title one gives to an adult who is a very important teacher."

The little boy caught on quickly. "What do you teach?" he asked warily.

The man clasped his fingers and laid his hands across his belly.

"Magic," he said, licking his lips to hide the smile. "Ooo?" gasped the child, his eyes widening. "Can we start now?"

"You must learn to wait," Crowley chid.

"Learn to wait *as well as*? Or lean to wait *instead of*?" was the cheeky reply.

This made the old man's face crack and a loud chortle escaped his lips. He gave the child a hug out of sheer happiness. He beamed at Stella and nodded his pride. For the first time since their arrival, she relaxed. She felt the tension go out of her back and she breathed more easily. Nothing had been said at all, but she had come here feeling as if she were on probation. She fathomed how crucial it was, not just to her but to the boy's future, that her efforts be approved. The man was pleased. She could let go at last.

She had called him Andrew, she explained, but Crowley announced that from here on his name would be Amado.

"It means: a gift of love," he declaimed.

The boy said it sounded more like an oven-cleaner — I was thinking of products called "Zebo" and "Zippo" — for a fire-lighter, and this made Aleister guffaw yet again.

He kept them up for several hours, plying them with questions and asking them to describe many little details. He was trying to fix a few points of reference. There was a seven year vacuum he needed to fill. In his eagerness he failed to notice the boy's fatigue, how his eyes dropped, how his limbs were like lead. It was Stella who finally pointed it out.

"He's half asleep," she said. "He's dropping in his tracks. Surely the rest can wait?"

Crowley picked him up and headed for the stairs. "Come, come, my little man, when you wake up and yawn tomorrow morning, it will be your birthday," he reminded. "I am the greatest magician, I can make your dearest wish come true, so what would you like for a present?"

"Could I have a sledge?" Amado asked.

"But... there is no snow."

"Then could I please have a sledge *and* snow?"

"He's mine," cried Crowley as he shook with mirth. "No doubt about it, he's mine."

He repeated it, or words to that effect, next day at a wonderful party where everybody wore colourful fancy dress. With all the egoism of a child, I thought this was my birthday party. It may well have been that too, of course, but it was actually my ritual presentation to certain of Crowley's followers and to the gods. The room was as big as a Baptist chapel. There was lots of singing and some funny games. There was one point where Aleister lifted him high in the air and they all stopped talking. "This child is mine," he said in voice like the vicar's at Evensong. "May you all bear witness. It is my will to proffer the Gods my own true son."

"My name is Amado," I told them all.

It was the only time he kissed me.

7
HOR-NUBTI

Horus, the vanquisher of evil

Neighbourliness
Looking back, I am still surprised that he didn't take more care. Things were never hidden. He had no concept of security. He just went about openly, letting everyone know who he was! I have a funny feeling there may have been some sense behind his madness. That flashy way he had did draw attention to him as a man; perhaps it worked the other way too, and drew the eye away from his actions. Now and again, you see, he did exercise his magical powers. No, he did not hold back from fulfilling his role as a Master, but somehow or other he managed to put screens around himself. You would never notice unless you were watching out for it. He was very clever at it. What I am really saying is that a lot of his behaviour served the same purpose as a conjuror's patter, the stall-holder's spiel, or the car salesman's flim-flam: it stopped people seeing what he didn't want them to see.

What with one thing and another, it wasn't difficult to recognize him and, wherever he went, people were always trying to have a word with him, get him in one corner, just to seek his help. If it was something he could do there and then without any great show or ceremony, then he'd do it. If something more was called for then either he'd say no, or else he'd see to it later, in private. In spite of all his alleged flamboyance, he didn't like to cause any 'fuss or palaver'. Nobody was given an outright refusal. They all went away at least partly satisfied.

By adopting this approach, he never caused anyone the slightest offence. He didn't ask for money, and when they pressed it on him, as country folk will, he gave them a name of someone who needed it: a young widow with three children, an old man who needed food, and so on. I never saw money actually change hands.

When I went back there, many years later, people still remembered him. They pretended deafness until I told them who I was. Then they told me quietly how he was remembered for his kindness and his "little ways of working things." He would be proud, I think, to have been remembered by them with such fondness and gratitude.

"It is always a temptation to show off," he said, ruffling my hair. "And not just while you are young, either. That is all very well if you are selling pots of hedgehog grease. You must convince the crowd it will cure all ills — everything from haemorrhoids to noisy neighbours! In that case, you see, a touch of razzle-dazzle and a sprinkle of rainbow-dust wouldn't go amiss."

He fixed me with a stern eye and shook his head. "But that's not how magic is done! Forget your tricks. Never do it for cheers or a bit of cheap applause. Go slowly. Do it calmly. Try to copy nature. Otherwise..." his voice dropped down to his boots "... you might catch the eye of a stranger!"

Hey Presto!
He judged by my face that I didn't understand. He tried to explain. "There is a common superstition," he said, "never to light three cigarettes from one match. It started during the Great War, the war to end all wars! We're less naive about it now so we call it the First World War. Anyway the idea went about that enemy snipers were alerted by the striking of the match for the first cigarette. They took careful aim by the second. When it reached the third, they pulled the trigger!" Aleister grimaced a bit sadly. "It's much the same with magic except we're not talking about matches, cigarettes nor rifles. There is an enemy though. They have got their snipers out. Any little display or any roll of drums — your tinsel rituals attract them like flies. It's lonely out there in the void. It's boring doing nothing. It's very nice of you to give them a target to attack."

He lifted his massive shoulders and gave a careless shrug. "It is never very clever to let people see how you obtain your results," he said. "It doesn't much matter whether you've used real magic or a little light legerdemain — if they think they get it, they will try to repeat it. It's almost as bad as doing tricks for a children's birthday party." He snorted a laugh. "Let them dream it was a miracle, as indeed it often is... but always leave them just enough room to doubt. Never impress them too much, my boy. They'll never forgive you. Remember that, whatever else you forget. Never drive people into a corner and oblige them to believe. It's a crime and you'd have to pay for it!"

This was not the only time he tried to drum it into me that there were dangers in occultism. He thought too many people ignored the risks they took. At one time, I even heard him say that he was sorry he had ever allowed the Golden Dawn Rituals to be published at all. "Not that they were wholly real," he explained. "But the Gods alone know how many minds have cracked like walnuts and the soul sucked out." He saw my horrified expression and patted my shoulder. "Didn't you know?" he asked. "That's how the term nut-case began — and after that it changed into crackers."

I can't judge whether the locals viewed him as just an eccentric, or whether they saw something more special in him. They made full use of his powers anyway. You can never tell with country folk; was it a case of double insurance, doing it just to make sure? He was never reluctant as long as they obeyed his little rules: no photos, no strangers, and no blabbing in the pub. He cleaned unlucky orchards as if they were wounds from a car accident. He repaired sick cows just as if they were bicycles with bent wheels. As for old ladies, they got "a little something" in their tea. In other words, he bluffed them. Or to be more accurate: he did nothing that might offend or insult whatever religious beliefs they had.

He never told them he was using magic. Instead, he talked about old ways and country ways and the ways of the wise from long ago.

If a family fell on hard times, he'd whisper the name of a horse in the husband's ear. Always round the corner, round the back, never where anyone would overhear. In all his good work, and I believe it was good work, he made sure there was never a witness. This, mind you, from the same man who stopped at nothing to grab some publicity!

Folkestone Meet

During the very first visit we often ate late in the evening. Afterwards, we would just sit around and he would play idly with his chess, while my mam reminisced gently. She was good at it too. She told stories about her past as if she were directing them for the unseen cameras. She wandered of course, the way one does, and jumped from one subject to another that seemed a thousand miles away. She explained how my grandma had been a Gipsy. Fondly, she told the story of that romantic meeting, forty-odd years before, when she met her future husband at Doncaster Races. "He loved horses," she murmured. "Above all, he enjoyed betting on them. He and his brothers would even bet on which fly would get to the piece of sugar first," she laughed. "He used to tell me: 'I'd rather win money than work down a coal-mine'," and she laughed. "I've not been very often myself, but I was always excited."

"Then we must go again," he announced. "There's a meet coming up at Folkestone. High time the lad was introduced to the so-called sport of Kings!"

My memories of that day are a whirl of colourful crowds and strange noises. So much was new, so much was strange, my mind couldn't cope and I felt bemused. I went about like someone in a daze. An old man strode up to Crowley, humbly dressed, with a flat-cap and an old muffler knotted round his neck. They exchanged a few words and seemed on good terms. "My dear," said Crowley, calling to my Mam who was by the paddock rails. When she turned, she was dumb-struck. "Hello, lass," said the old man. He half smiled and sucked his lips in. "My best regards to thy mam." He lifted me up and studied me with pale blue eyes. "You're a right one," he said with a grin, "gambling already at your age." My mam pulled herself together and laid her hand softly on his arm. "How have you been?" she asked softly. "Are you all right?"

"Oh I'm doing nicely," he replied. "Very nicely, all taken into account." His eyes flicked toward AC who gave a tiny nod. "I live close by. Nice couple. Three young lads. I've got my own little room in the cottage."

"I'll come to see you."

"Best not. Not yet a while. You could write though. I'd be fair glad. Happen you could send me a picture of the lad?" I didn't pay much attention but afterward, on our way home, she squeezed my hand till it hurt. "That was your grandad," she gasped and began to cry softly.

AC patted her hand. "He is fine," he told her kindly. "We keep an eye on him."

We were too moved to even think of asking how Crowley had even found the old man. I learned later that my grandad moved to the coalfields in Kent, after my grandma left him. He'd made friends there. Retired there. And then one day this Crowley chap came looking for him. "Said I was his father-in-law all but for some confetti." I suppose I should remember too that my grandad was of noble birth too... all but for a bit of the same confetti. But somehow, I don't think that was Aleister's reason. He was just doing good as he saw it.

The Dovecot
In the end, we did go and see him in his little cottage, of course. He was thrilled to bits, as if he was showing us off to his friends. He took us all walking. It was his favourite pastime and though he'd never read a single book on the subject, so far as we knew, he could give a running lecture on every plant or insect that we saw. He may have been jealous and bad-tempered when he was young but he certainly loved nature. I lagged behind, or went on ahead, because they had such a lot to talk about. Names that meant nothing to me: who had married whom, who had died, how many children there were all told... with a lot of chuckling they told me I had a hundred and thirty two cousins. They proved it after on a bit of paper.

As I circled round them, roaming like a gundog, I found a smallish old castle with a dovecot in the grounds. I had not the slightest idea what this strange building could be. My mam and grandad caught me up and he started to explain that in olden days it was like having a fish-pond or a refrigerator — fresh meat always at hand. "There are no doves now though."

"Yes there are," I said. "Look!" I pointed at a fluttering cloud of birds so white, it looked as if someone had shaken an apple tree and all the blossom was tumbling down. A lady was there, wearing a long pale dress. She was throwing seed to the birds.

My grandfather was looking at me with ice-blue eyes. My mam held on to his arm. "He does that," she murmured, and then a pause. "There's nowt wrong with him though."

"No," said my grandad; staring toward the lady and the doves. "Nowt wrong at all."

Back at the cottage, the three boys of the house played with me. We climbed a huge tree, all three together, and because I wasn't used to it, I fell. Down I plummeted, bouncing from branch to branch, and ended up with one leg hanging over some barbed wire fencing. But apart from a slight graze, I wasn't hurt.

In the old garage-cum-workshop, there were lots of old tools and bits of broken down cars. We had found some unused bullets on an army practice range and now we intended to prise the bullets out of the cartridge case and extract the powder. Stupidly we tried holding one in a vice. It went off and shot through the roof. Again, I had just a graze on my right index finger.

Finally, out of pure mischief, the biggest lad, Jim, made me hold some wires from a thing called a magneto. The other two were chuckling up their sleeve and backed away. He turned a handle rapidly but nothing happened. He came over to touch me and he was flung across the shed so that he crashed through the door.

When we got back home to Yorkshire, we started receiving unusual gifts from Kent. A crate of apples one week, a sack of chestnuts another. We even got a box of oysters with seaweed dripping out. When the war came and food-rationing began, these things were very precious to us. At school, I could have been ostracised as a scholarship boy. Instead, I was now very popular. My satchel was stuffed with fruit of one sort or another, and I used to sell them at lunch-time. One penny for an apple, two pence for a dozen nuts.

8
SHU

The god of air or emptiness deified

Romney Marshes
My occult training began the very next day of our first meeting. I didn't notice because none of it felt the least bit like school. "I give my lessons on the trot," he said. "I think better when I'm moving. That may be why I used to climb mountains!" At school, thinking-caps were worn only when sitting silently. One couldn't do two things at the same time, they said. Now here was my father preaching the opposite, and I found out later in life that he was right. Busy the lower brain with some routine task and the higher brain is freed. Women know this. They solve all their problems by having a good knit.

Aleister loved chess. He tried hard — too hard — to get me interested and only made me loathe it. How poetic when, thirty-odd years later, Gerald Yorke offered me the very same chess-set as a keepsake! It was his equivalent of Sherlock Holmes' violin. Imagine: he even took it out at meal times! We could leave the table without him knowing. We'd just leave him there, picking a chicken to shreds. I was only seven, of course, and I had my own kind of wonder. So what I remember might seem trivial to others. The names of places or streets never stuck because they were no more important to me then than telephone numbers today. But there is one thing I'll never forget: the small gauge railway that runs across the Romney Marshes from Hythe to Dimchurch and Dungeness. I had just seen the film "Doctor Syn" in which George Arliss played the role of "Scarecrow" — a vicar by day, a smuggler by night. Aleister, on the other hand, gave me a lecture on how they reclaimed land from the sea and used windmills to pump the water out. It was the one and only time that he really bored me.

Later on, we left the train and went walking through the sticky marshes. He stopped by a small pond and raised his hat.

"Good day," he said politely.

The game puzzled me. "Who are you talking to?"

"To that tadpole. He's called Tommy."

I was totally mystified. I wanted to laugh but dare not.

"How do you know he's called Tommy?" I asked.

"Things are whatever I choose to call them."

I blinked a moment and frowned. "Is that why I'm Amado now?"

"You were always Amado."

He spoke with such great self-assurance. He was not playing the clown. He could persuade adults, let alone a child, to suspend their disbelief and join in with him. There was no need for circus make-up. In fact, he wore a silk hat, a frock-coat and a pin-stripe trousers. He looked like a bank manager. But he had no need to act a role, he just became someone else. Oh yes, he could be funny and loved acting the goat. He was discreet though. The jokes were never risqué — not until I was older.

I was still concerned about this tadpole though. "Animals and things haven't got names," I argued. "They can't talk and so they don't need them."

"But we can talk, and we need to call them something," he smiled. "So whatever we call them, that is what they become. A tadpole is not a tadpole as far as it is concerned. But it is kind enough not to object when I use that word as a label. That way, my boy, we can overcome the barriers of distance and time and haul it out of the darkness... by its name."

He dipped his hand in the water and scooped the tiny creature on to the dusty land. "We can kill things by means of their name."

I flicked the writhing black comma back into the pond. "And there you are," said Crowley. "You have saved its life because I called it Tommy."

Tadpoles

I wasn't at all sure I understood, but I got a funny itchy feeling. "It's like two worlds," I mused, "and our minds can walk between them because we know the password."

"Not just our minds," he said with a smile. "Look," he tossed a stone in to the pond. "Our world is open and boundless. Theirs is more like Switzerland, except the Swiss get much less fun from life."

"I like the Swiss," I retorted. I was thinking of Shirley Temple in a film called 'Heidi'.

"Don't be absurd," he snapped. "The Swiss don't even like themselves! There is a theory that they are all clockwork penguins. They have about the same amount of emotion in any case. If you visit one of their cemeteries, there is an overpowering resemblance to a row of bank-vaults." He smiled but his eyes were glacial. "In short, no, I do not like them. God knows, I've tried. I still blame Hannibal: far too reckless with those damned elephants!" He chuckled and gave me a familiar nudge. "Don't take me so seriously, lad. Some of my best friends are Swiss but, like garlic dressing on a vampire's salad, they're not entirely to my taste."

I've no idea why he was so bitter about the Swiss. Another time he said that once they had founded the Red Cross, the Swiss felt excused from doing any other act of kindness. "They are a nation of devout egoists!" he said. I often wonder if some Swiss friend had refused to lend him money. At any rate, as regards certain subjects he was like a dog with a bone: he just went on and on.

I didn't listen to him. My mind wandered off in a daydream. "Tadpoles change," I heard myself say in a funny voice. Aleister stopped dead in his tracks. "I beg your pardon?" he asked, looking at me oddly. "What did you say?" he repeated softly.

"Their little mountain world will have a ring of fire around it."

He nodded wisely as if what I said made sense. I didn't even know why I had said it. "Anything else?" he asked. The noise of the sea came back, not that I'd heard it fade before. I looked at him with a vague sense of panic in my stomach. "I think I'm going to be sick," I murmured. "Can we go?"

"It's just the jolt," he said. "You'll not be sick!" and we continued our walk along the edge of the sea, heading back for the station.

"You know," he explained carefully, "the lower down the ladder, the less a creature is aware of self or even of its own existence. At the middle levels though, animals begin to have a sense of 'us' or 'our kind', and 'them' or the 'other kind'. They seem to know what and who represents a threat to their own species." He spoke quite slowly, with lots of pauses, as if he were picking his words with infinite care. "Nature," he went on, "is a sort of melting-pot. It makes and then re-makes the players in the great game of survival. It's almost as though the gods were still developing the rules of the game," he murmured, fingering his chess-set. "And this poor wretch called man, he thinks he is a problem asking to be solved. He just doesn't realize that he was meant to be an answer."

Cliff Path

He'd shown me pictures of the famous cliffs, the Seven Sisters, and announced that the number seven was important to me. He said that the cliffs of Dover were well worth looking at. What's more, there was a castle on top. Postcards are all very well, but I was eager to look with my own eyes. I was aghast at their sheer size. Looked at from below, they looked harmless enough, but once you were on top, looking down, the effect was a hundred times worse. "What are you scared of?" asked Crowley in a humorous voice. "It's chalk," I stammered, "just chalk! If we go too near the edge it might crumble and then we'd fall."

"In that case, we'll take one of the paths a little further down that leads to St. Margaret's Bay."

If anything this was worse. Now I couldn't even retreat from the edge because of the white wall behind me. I clung to it as closely as I could.

"You and I, my boy, we can walk the wind if we so choose." It's interesting now to remember that "Wind-walker," like "star-watcher," is one of those dummy names that country folk use to avoid referring to a magician directly. He pointed toward the sea. "You must to learn to recognize doors and gateways when they present themselves. They are the only way that one may travel between this world here and that world there." He didn't like to speak of "the other world" which carried overtones of "the life hereafter" or the "dear departed." Indeed, to be perfectly accurate, he would draw the distinction between "this world here and now" and "that world there and then."

I must admit that this way of speaking puzzled me a lot and it left me way behind. He knew it, and it didn't worry him. I think he was getting me used to it, rather than explaining it. At the start I imagined that 'this world here' meant England, while 'that world there' meant France. He must have caught my thoughts because he chuckled softly and gave my hair a ruffle.

Then he said "Ah-ha!" and he chin pointed like a gun-dog toward the path, a few score yards further ahead. Walking toward us were two small figures, dressed in black, with white wings on their heads. The wind was making their robes flutter.

"What are they?" I asked, taken aback by their odd clothing. "Nuns," he said, with a certain relish, the way that a stork might whisper "frogs."

They were Sisters of Mercy, of course, but those large white coifs gave their head a certain triangular shape. "They look a bit like penguins," I muttered.

"In which case," hissed my father, "we'll kill two birds with one stone."

He grasped my hand firmly in his and marched me forward with a bold stride. We took up the greater part of the path's width.

Although their eyes were cast down modestly, the two sisters had clearly remarked our presence. One dropped back, like a well-drilled soldier, to take up a position behind the other. They kept coming toward us but now their eyes darted nervously to the drop on their left.

My father squeezed my hand with delight. "We seem to be at an impasse," he said aloud to me.

Vertigo

Then he faced the sisters, broad, beaming and benign. "Good morning to you, sisters," he boomed in his best baritone. "What a fine day for a pensive stroll." His voice carried that certain bonhomie which a spider might use when greeting two plump flies.

"Good morning, sir." said the one in front. "It is indeed a splendid day, thank God."

"We are going to the shops," piped in the other from behind. "We need to purchase some supplies."

The conversation sounded more and more like an extract from a pantomime — the bit where Little Red Riding Hood talks to the Wolf.

Crowley looked from one to the other in pretended amazement. "And do you two frail ladies always take this difficult and dangerous route?"

"It is very much shorter," said one in front.

"And we very rarely meet anyone" added the one behind.

"But your hats or veils," smiled Crowley kindly, "are spread like seagull's wings. The slightest gust of naughty wind could lift you off your feet and plunge you to the violent sea below."

The sea was as still as a mill pond, nor was there so much as a whisper of wind. But Crowley didn't let this stop him, and neither did it prevent the nuns' rosy cheeks from taking on an apple-green tinge. "We trust in the good Lord, sir." "How very correct and virtuous, ladies. However, here and now we are face to face with a slight problem. How do we go our opposite ways without causing any distress? No cause for anxiety, I assure you. It is we who must cede passage to you."

So saying, he grasped my hand tightly and walked me off the edge of the cliff. I describe events exactly as they happened. There was no preamble, no magic formula. Quite literally, we just walked out as if the surface of the path had some sort of invisible extension. And we stood there, our feet in midair, as he raised his hat and gave a courtly bow. The two sisters seemed to have taken root. They both boggled at our shoes and let out a series of little yelps and whimpers.

"Sisters!" chided Crowley regretfully, "didn't your mother teach you to say thank you?"

The nuns just hoiked up their skirts and ran.

My own jaw was clamped tight shut. Even when we were back on the solid path, I couldn't speak. "Oh do cheer up," he grumbled. "I simply took you through a door, that is all. Since you didn't understand, you had to be shown. As for those two dear nuns, it's the most exciting thing that's ever happened to them and as from today they will be ten times more holy."

The fact that I too was still paralysed by fear seemed only to irritate him. "Shall we do it again?" he snapped. "No," I yelled.

He put his arm round my shoulder with a grim smile. "Oh dear!" he murmured. "Oh what a shame!" He gave me a hearty squeeze. "All unwittingly, I believe I have sparked off a dreadful fear of heights. It is just about the only thing I can feel no sympathy for.

Knew a fella once — started gibbering on the stairs in Harrod's. Another one used to hop about like a scalded cock whenever he went near an airplane. Worst of all was a poor chap called Digby — used to get it whenever he had an orgasm. I hope you'll not suffer as badly as he."

"What's an orgasm?" I asked naively.

He sucked in his cheeks and his eyes twinkled. "Just another name for vertigo!"

In spite of his good wishes, I've suffered from vertigo most of my life!

9
BENNU

*A sacred bird, born in Arabia, not unlike the phoenix.
It appears once in five hundred years*

Monotheism
The three world religions don't view themselves as equal. They behave like distant cousins waging a feud that is often bloodier than that between enemy states. Their creed orders them to be charitable, and yet for centuries each has tried merrily to butcher the others with a barbarity worthy of Attila the Hun. In spite of this, they stick to the old, insane logic. There is only one god. If this people adore one God, and that people also adore one God then... both those peoples are worshipping the same god. They are brothers. And they loathe one another.

"There's a flaw in their logic," quipped Crowley. "Nobody has proven there is only one god. Suppose there are more?" He smiled like someone about to checkmate. "And if there are more, how can any religion be sure it has chosen the right one? What if they've all picked the loser, as in the Grand National?" His laughter rumbled like a storm in the offing. "In any case, if they know they are right, why are they so damn touchy about rivals?"

He would have no truck with any of them. "Belief in one god restricts individual liberty," he remarked. "You can do anything, justify everything, in the name of your one God. 'Cry: God for Harry, England and Saint George,' and then slaughter the French. 'God bless America', and wipe out the Viet-cong. That's what most of it's about: not reverence but power, not belief but loyalty!" He sniffed heavily, and rubbed his nose with a florid handkerchief.

"Next best thing, I suppose — Queen and Country! But a very inferior kind of 'next best thing'. A true God would let each person seek and find. Not religion though. It tells you what to believe, which is to say: the party-line. No deviation either. If you let one get away with it, they might all try."

"Very good for faith to burn a few heretics alive. Tends to turn one vegetarian." He smiled and gave a depreciating 'humph' that was mid-way between a chuckle and a heave of nausea.

"Their theology states that each man has free will, yet they try to control his life and his mind. Worse still, they make each family responsible for its children and each man responsible for his brother. You're not free if you follow a religion. You live in an observation ward."

He reviled the Christian church, and not only for the rigid views his parents had held. They had been of the Plymouth Brethren and kept its rules down to the letter. They were too vigorous when they tried to ram the gospels down his throat and he rebelled. He did not blame God for his parents' errors though. As a young man he had no strong opinions except that he could not tolerate the churches. In short, the scars on his heart did not oppress his intellect at all. He became derisive of any "one-God show", and argued quite cogently that they were "a clarion call that mustered recruits for evil". But even though he derided all three of the world faiths, he was especially scornful of the Jews.

Paganism

When Greece and Rome, fathers of European culture, used the word 'pagan', they saw no connection with evil, human sacrifice, wanton carousal or the worship of many gods. Such things were so common everywhere else, they hardly deserved a special mention. Pagan just meant rustic, yokelish and uncouth. The great cities were made of stone and marble whereas the country was all hovels, straw roofs and rough living. Bumpkins as compared to city sophisticates. Since they were indeed master of the known world, the Romans had good reason to feel that they had got their religion right! They believed in many gods and so did all the other early city states.

Israel, of course, was not a civilization. But then, it hadn't always been a one-god system either. Previously, before the Garden of Eden, Jehovah was husband to a goddess called Lilith. She was depicted or symbolized as a stone pillar. This tells us something about the frequent reference to stones in the bible. People were being stoned to death, people were striking stones and opening up fountains, others were tying stones round their necks and flinging themselves into the sea, and then there were angels, rolling stones across the mouths of tombs. Crowley said there was more in this than met the eye.

As Judaism developed, the goddess Lilith was demoted. First she became Adam's former wife, and then she left him to be the consort of Lucifer. What you might call — 'a fallen woman'. But now one understands why Lot's wife, looking back to witness the downfall of Sodom and Gomorrah, was punished by being changed into a pillar of salt. An inexplicable event unless you know what that pillar truly represented. These shifts in Jewish theology were mirrored in the organization of Jewish society. As the goddess was displaced, so the feminine role in Jewish political life was diminished. To compensate her slightly, Jewish home life would rotate around "Mama", and Jewish "blood" would descend via the woman rather than the man.

"Judaism," said my father, "was founded by a rebel, Adam. Christ rebelled against Judaism and is called the *second Adam*. Mohammed was a rebel against the Christian heresy of Bishop Nestorius. There you have it in a nutshell: three rebels and three creeds. Three plaited concepts of good and evil, reward and punishment, and heaven and hell. And isn't this the true origin, the genesis, of the devil? Once you invent Old Nick," Aleister sneered, "you open the prospect of traffic with him, of going over to his side, and of apostasy."

He was serious in arguing that monotheism fostered revolt and that the three faiths were the god-fathers of Communism. "Karl Marx, and Leon Trotsky were both born Jews," he said pithily. "You see how naive it is to relate Black Magic with devil-worship or Satanism?"

He knew many wicked people. We even went to watch one of their rituals, as I describe below. In my turn, I too know some Luciferans and the like but I leave them to it. It isn't worth the trouble trying to explain it to them. Either they were venting spleen or else making a mint of money but they are just about as effective as the lads with spray-cans who feel fulfilled only if they disfigure some public building.

If one goes to the lengths of worshipping the devil, one is just like any other naughty boy spitting at his mother and scribbling across his father's football pools. One is seeking revenge.

It only gets dangerous when it is mixed with politics. As it very often is!

The Devil
In my opinion, writers and film makers are often guilty of sowing the seeds of evil by depicting new types of depravity, and dwelling on it in too great detail. It makes me smile to think how much Aleister Crowley and moral activists would have in common when you look behind the veils and smoke-screens!

"The Devil is the outcome of the way they define their God," he would explain. "One True God is necessary in order for the devil to rebel. So all those ninnies out there who freeze their arses off by bowing before the God of Evil can only justify it by first agreeing that the One True God exists! What would be the point of spitting on the cross if it offended nobody? You cannot commit an outrage if there is no one to be outraged. In other words, it is the presence of God alone that makes their mischief valid."

He sat back then, looking rather pleased at the way that he had put it.

"Just imagine," he went on. "If the Devil were God, there would be no Black Magic! It's because the devil is *not* god that Black Magic has any point and purpose."

"Then why don't they see this?" I asked shrewdly.

"Because they are blind! Because they need to flirt with danger! Because they follow a kind of unreason which is only a step away from what you and I call madness!" He shook his head with pity.

"Life has not dealt kindly with them. They are people who have suffered and endured sadness, and often they have achieved no great success in life. They are filled with bile and bitterness. They have tasted wormwood and gall. In their despair they turn toward the devil. They ask for vengeance. They beseech him to overturn the natural order of things and give them satisfaction at last. Whatever price is asked, it will seem a bargain to them."

I think he spoke the truth. People who have lapsed from a religion will turn again to God if they are struck by adversity. But people who suffered unjustly while they were believers will turn against their God and try to betray Him. One comes across black magic from time to time. Certain newspapers make sensational revelations every two or three years. Teenagers are "rescued" by distraught parents with the aid of an American minister. Most of this kind of stuff is pathetic and funny. I've met many "friends of Satan" or "lovers of Lucifer". The most memorable thing about them was their giggles. I've heard those same giggles in psychiatric hospitals, in the closed wards.

Kids go through a stage like this. Round about the age of ten, they enter a short period of mindless horror and filth. I was a vampire myself for a whole week, after seeing Bela Lugosi as Dracula. How I envied the black cloak with its red silk lining. How I longed to get my own back on my headmaster! But I soon moved on to better heroes. Those who don't may never mature. They will go on chasing their juvenile dreams of power. Who but the lonely and hungry are drawn to the red-light district?

I have no doubt that wicked people exist. Many of them have lost touch with reality. It slid from their fingers. Now they imagine they can reduce creation to chaos again — an urge which looks well in Nazi uniform and sporting a swastika. Like the Mafia, black magic yearns for power but hates to serve it. The same difference as between Nietzsche's "glory of Will" and the Law of Thelema's emphasis on love. Oh what a risky game they play! Black magic is not so much a religion as an occult whoopee cushion. "It vexes," said Crowley. "It causes a nuisance. But all it's good for is a pastime for louts!"

Former Friends
Dennis Wheatley[1] knew my father very well. They often dined at each other's house and there was a certain collaboration during the Second World War, which I explore more deeply later on. When Wheatley wrote his 'black magic novels' — 'The Devil Rides Out', 'To the Devil a Daughter' etc — he picked Crowley's brains for some of the background detail. At least two of his novels were turned into successful films. I knew him, mainly through correspondence, and in his old age I was sad to see how he tried to renounce his past and denounce Crowley. In a late book, he had nothing good to say at all. Let me give a few examples:

> "...For some years, Crowley lived in Sicily, with a number of male and female disciples at the Abbey of Thelema, near Cefalu. Black Masses were said there and animals offered up to Satan..."

Comment: Quite simply, there were no black masses. There were

---

1. Wheatley D. *The Devil and All His Works,* Hutchinson, 1971.

Gnostic masses but I doubt if Wheatley appreciated the difference. On one occasion only, a cat scratched Crowley which he chucked out of a room in fury. Because the cat was injured, the women told the men that they should put the cat out of its misery. That was the only time an animal was killed.

> "...Having had Crowley to dinner several times, I told my friend Z that although I found him interesting, I was convinced that he (Crowley) could not harm a rabbit. "Ah, not now," replied Z. "But he was different before that affair in Paris..."

Comment: The Paris workings took place in 1914. Hence, according to Wheatley, Crowley was a rabbit-lover from that date on i.e. for the remaining thirty-three years of his life in fact.

> "...The affair in Paris was as follows... Crowley had raised Pan all right. MacAleister was dead and Crowley, stripped of his magician's robes, a naked gibbering idiot crouching in a corner..."

Comment: the person referred to as MacAleister, was Victor Neuberg who died of tuberculosis in 1940 at the age of 57. Crowley didn't have the physique to be very fond of public nakedness. He was also a graduate of Cambridge, and as I remember, never suffered from any nervous or mental disorder in his life.

> "...You can follow the Left-hand Path, summed up in Aleister Crowley's precept 'Do what thou wilt is the whole of the law' — lie, steal, cheat; give free rein to all your basest instincts and commit any act of meanness or brutality, regardless of the misery it may cause others, in order to get what you want. Or you can follow the Right-hand path, summed up in the precept of Jesus Christ 'Love thy neighbour as thyself'..."

Comment: none at all except perhaps to mention that this comes rather ill from a man who is most well-known from having written about the devil in a most lurid and exciting way! When I wrote to Wheatley in some bitterness, he chose not to reply.

In direct contrast to all this, let me quote but one single statement from Kenneth Grant[2]:

> "...Crowley was the flower not only of the Golden Dawn — as Krishnamurti was the flower of the Theosophical Society — but of the entire body of Western occultism and its literature..."

Mr. Grant is the kind of friend most people would prefer.

---

2. Grant, K. *Outside the Circles of Time,* Frederick Muller, 1980.

10
NEBTHET

Goddess of the desert's edge or the fruitful and barren points at the edge of the Nile

Master Race

Black Masses were often recited in a building not far from Temple Bar in London. This was once the principal seat of the English Templars which is why it stood just within the protection of the city, and outside the grasp of Kings. If it wanted, the church could annul its centuries old expulsion of the Templars. It could even say it was sorry. Instead, it never mentions them. Not a whisper is spoken, not a prayer is uttered. The names of their dead do not appear in any calendar of saints nor on any list of martyrs. Why? Because it was Pope Clement V who agreed to let the Templars be tortured and burned[1] just as it was Pope Innocent III who gave orders for the Cathars to be slaughtered[2]. And was it not Pope Pius XII, just before the war, who hastily concluded a treaty with Hitler to ensure that church property would not be touched? The church always did have an equivocal attitude toward the Jews. "Whenever there's a struggle for power," commented Aleister, "it's always useful to have a victim available. Which is something the Catholic church has never been short of. Of course," he went on, "nobody in their right mind ever dared to criticise the church, much less contradict her. That was the quickest way of being condemned as a heretic and griddled in the market-place. But mark my words," he said. "When this war is over, just you watch what happens. The church will dance to a very different tune... always provided Germany loses, that is."

1. de Sede, G. *Les Templiers sont Parmi Nouse,* Paris, 1962.
2. de Rosa, P. **Vicars of Christ,** London 1989.

It might be thought that Crowley was racist or anti-Semitic. But no. He was not. He was totally against the Jewish religion though — mainly because of the errors it perpetuated. I realize it won't much comfort our Jewish friends, but he hated Islam and Christianity with just the same vehemence. He was quite catholic in his condemnation of all forms of monotheism, and the fanaticism which it usually engendered.

"Not that the Jews are entirely without blame," he went on, "though I would be labelled fascist for saying so. But who is more racist or bigoted than a Jew? What is the way they address their divinity: The Lord God of Abraham, Jacob and Isaac! The God of the Jews, in fact. No one else. It therefore follows, they claim, that the Jews are the chosen people of God. And there you have it. That is all there is to it. Even those with tickets may not board this bus because, poor sods, it is full both upstairs and down!"

Once he was on this subject, he often got angry. "You are a child and children are supposed to be unbiased: so open the Bible and run your eye through the Old Testament. It is one long list of gore and carnage. The horrors God committed to lend Israel a hand would make old Genghis Khan look like a lovable teddy bear! Catalogue the Hebrew triumphs and see how they were achieved: babies butchered at Passover, the fall of Babylon, Samson pulling down the temple on people's heads, and army after army massacred." He tilted his head and burst into his special voice. "The Assyrian came down like the wolf on the fold, and his cohorts were gleaming with purple and gold..."[3] He shook his head in a kind of brooding sorrow. "They talk about a Just God, a knowing God, but never mention equality or speak of fair play." He probed his denture with his tongue and sucked away an irritant crumb. "Interesting to recall," he observed, "that the Jews invented the 'Master Race' before Hitler was born."

Ancient Powers

It is a rather shocking idea, I agree. But no one then knew about the concentration camps nor about "the final solution". In any case, his mind shot off in a different direction.

"Moses was a curious chap — took on the court magicians of

---

3. Bryon *The Destruction of Sennacherib*.

Egypt and thrashed the poor sods. Hit a rock with his staff and water came gushing out. Used to have little wayside chats with burning bushes and what have you." He stared at the wall, no doubt looking beyond it. "A most High Magician, by all accounts; or so the Jews thought and most of Europe agreed. Cabalism or the magic of Moses, was at its very zenith during the Mediaeval period." He frowned at this point, as if the taste were sour. "Alchemy, I think you'll find, comes from 'al kimia': the art of turning one metal into another!"

Being the chosen people, he said, was as good for your morale as having a thousand fans chanting slogans and urging the team along. It was, after all, the only bit of optimism that the Jews possessed — what with bondage in Babylon, slavery in Egypt, hard times under the yoke of Rome and finally the great dispersion all over Europe. They hadn't a lot to sing about, neither then nor ever since. The need grew more urgent so the magic talisman was polished and gilded. The concept of "the chosen people" became the cornerstone of the Jewish faith. If any Jew had doubts, he stopped being a Jew.

I am no more Christian than my father was, but I feel a certain concern for those who are. The errors and pitfalls that I perceive in their lives are mostly due to ideas which they inherited from Judaism. It was only a tribal creed but it became ossified by events of history. There have been no new prophets in the last two thousand years, just the weary, endless wait. Oh yes indeed, they have suffered a great deal. But as the scriptures establish, and events in modern Israel witness, they are utterly capable of giving as good as they get.

"Being a Jew," said Crowley in a brutal epigram, "is all to do with foreskins and prawns. A joke in very bad taste, I dare say, but it has the ring of the name of a pub." His laughter rumbled to a halt when I didn't join in. "Oh don't look so woe-begone! You'll understand it better in a few years time and then you'll laugh."

I never did though... laugh, that is.

Ethnic religion is a local thing, a tribal response to the magical urge. The negro people, for example, were the "Celts of Africa". They were conquered, uprooted and enslaved. They were not brought simply because there was no market for them. It was the colonies that needed them as a cheap form of energy. The black slaves were thrashed as necessary, but otherwise stuffed with the gospel. They were conquered, uprooted and enslaved. They were not brought simply because there was no market for them. It was the colonies that needed them as a cheap form of energy. The black slaves were thrashed as necessary, but otherwise stuffed with the gospel. They were being taught their place. Of course, their original beliefs flowered in secret and learned how to express themselves under the guise of the cross. Hence, when the slaves were freed, those old beliefs rose to the surface quickly in the form of Voodoo here, Umbanda and Condomble there, and Santeria somewhere else.[4]

The down-trodden negro never sought the status of White Men. What their religion expresses is a simple yearning for harmony between the two worlds. "The bishops could learn a lot from the negro," laughed Aleister, "but God help the man who suggests it. On the other hand, the Negro could learn still more about the ancient power they possess, if only they would stop thinking like ex-slaves."

The Great Beast

"What did I do?" He would rant in feigned grief, beating his chest in the wanton gestures of silent films. "What did I do to merit their censure? Was it I who declared holy wars? Am I the one who sent off the children on their doomed Crusade? Was it me who tortured old crones and burnt heretics in the public square? No! Not me, not Nero, not the Huns — but the Popes! Did the Holy Spirit envelop its head with one wing, or did it approve the tyranny? Did you know," he asked in a shocked voice, "that the Vatican has the biggest network of spies in the entire world? And did you know," he continued, "one dare not describe some of their heinous acts without being called a liar?"

"So why baptise me the most evil man who ever lived?" He prowled the carpet as if being paid to test it. "When my mother, in despair, accused me of being The Great Beast of the Bible, I agreed. But why did she do that? Can you guess? Because she caught me playing with myself and that rocked her faith in God."

"Oh the sin, the shame, the stigma and the disgrace! She had never seen anything like it in her life. She was so stunned and so

---

4. McGregor, P. *The Moon and Two Mountains,* 1966 Souvenir Press, London.

sickened, at first she couldn't find a word evil enough. God knows she tried all the ones she could lay her tongue to: villain, wretch, monster, hellion — and then screeched her ultimate anathema."

"Spawn of Satan," she howled, "Great Beast of the apocalypse!"

"Then in hell's name," I shrieked, "what do we call the dam that suckled me?" I gave her a deep, cold, furious bow and hissed "The Whore of Babylon, I believe?"

"A hit, a very palpable hit! That got her! That really struck home. I kept on saying it. I repeated it over and over again till she just frothed at the mouth." He let his head fall. "In the end I was just laughing at myself in wry and tragic mockery. It was a joke that went on too long." He blinked his eyes once or twice very quickly, and then he smiled. "Perhaps it was wrong of me to have said it. It may well be I should have struck her instead." He gave a tiny shrug and sighed. "But she winced, though! Oh yes. She winced."

The shock I felt must have been visible on my face. "You are lucky, my lad. So are all boys whose mothers love them." He gave me a warm hug. "To your Mam you are a blessing, whereas to mine I was a challenge, sent by God, to test her integrity. Nevertheless, I have done nothing that measures up to deeds done by pleasant, pious people in the name of God. It will all be repeated within your own lifetime, just mark my words. Protestant, Catholic, Muslim, Hindu and Jew: each and every one of them capable of being a ravening beast or a howling devil. Yet each will say he was created in God's image. If that were true, they should be terrified to meet Him." He shook his head in deep anguish. "A modicum of doubt from time to time is quite salutary for the soul." "What with God and Anti-god," he laughed harshly, "the Leftists of the world should all join together in thanking religion for the great, unifying force that it gave."

"I give you three warnings," he swore. "The Jewish war will be with gold. The Islamic war will be with blood. The Christian war will be with guilt." He thrust out his bottom lip, bringing Mussolini to mind.

"And I'll tell you something else," he added. "The direst words to be found in world literature: 'The Prince of Darkness is a Gentleman'!"[5]

5. Shakespeare, *King Lear* 3 IV 139.

Calumny

Just because so many writers refer to Crowley as "that infamous black magician" does not make it true. They are doing what writers have always done: forgetting that they started the myth themselves. It is after all an old technique. "Excuse me, Prime Minister. Rumour has it that..." or "Lord Archbishop, many people believe that..." They are not really asking a question. They are provoking their victim into making an unguarded reply. They are trying to catch him on the hop. We used to do the same thing at school: "Which hand do you wipe your bottom with? Left or right? Ooo, you dirty bugger," we'd shriek. "At our house we all use paper." It just goes to show that all writers were once children, and some of them still are.

But the serious ones, the better ones, know better than to play this kind of silly game. Those newspapers that do not deal with news — they are the only ones who try to keep this kind of raggedy old shuttle-cock in the air. Them and the authors who need the money. The men of honour are different. I'm only surprised that they have never protested or done anything to rectify the wrong. Some of them knew Crowley. One or two would even count themselves as his friends. Apart from the intrepid Kenneth Grant, how many have shown the loyalty he had the right to expect?

In the next few pages or so, it may seem that I don't treat the subject seriously. In fact, I am doing my best to present the attitude my father showed. He wasn't always serious either. Very far from it. I tell the story exactly as it happened and I can't change it just to win approval. It may not seem very sensible, but you can be sure I have my reasons.

11
ANPU

*The jackal-headed god who conducts souls to the
Land of the dead: inventor of funerary rites*

Trinity Church

For some perverse reason, the church had been built on the side of a hill and the need to orient it toward the east or whatever had made the job doubly difficult. They had done their best though. They made a hole into the hill at one end and by shifting the muck to the other end, they created a level site on a kind of artificial terrace. So far, it hadn't slipped, but it looked in imminent danger of doing so.

Round the back though, if indeed a church can be said to have a front and a back, the terrain fell away sharply and under the great east window, the wall of the crypt was exposed to public view. Not only that — there was a huge iron gate through which one could peer into the dark and echoing interior. The metal-work was incredibly rusty, almost eaten through in places. But the hinges were well-oiled, and the padlock was new.

"Have you got a key?" I asked.

"No. In any case, we don't want to put them on their guard."

"But how do we get in?"

Crowley winked. "We use the door inside the church."

I thought about this for a moment and then I asked "Why don't they do that?"

He sneered and gave a humph. "Not as impressive!"

He led me back, up the steep slope and past some tilting graves with daffodils on. "White magic," he explained, "goes about its business discreetly. It doesn't want to draw attention to itself or cause anyone the slightest fear or apprehension. In short, my lad: white magic does not set its sights on dominating the world." He paused to get his breath back and held on to a drain-pipe.

"But black magic is the exact opposite. It likes both secrecy and show — a bit like a Hollywood film-star." He winked and gave a little smile. "That's where I let myself down: I'm a white magician but also an exhibitionist! But genuine black magic wants to lure others in and ensnare them in its leathery wings. It uses anxiety, it infects people with terror, and it seeks to topple the world. The next time you meet a black magician, have a good look at his eyes. They are fanatical. They are the eyes of one who longs to dominate and control. They train to be puppet-masters!" As we turned into the porch he said something else that was odd. "Always notice how people open doors," he advised. "It tells you a lot about their character."

We advanced into the nave trying to go quietly, but our feet clanged against the flagstones, and the inset brass grills down the main aisle seemed to resonate with voices. In no great hurry, Aleister looked around with the eye of a connoisseur. He was still chewing on the indigestible fact — that he was known as a black magician, a satanist or devil-worshipper. To the best of my knowledge, he was nothing of the sort, and he himself denied it vigorously. A real black magician wouldn't have cared twopence.

"I had a classical education," he snorted. "When I say Demon I mean what the ancient Greeks meant: *Daimon* or an indwelling spirit of nature. Those bigots know it too. But they are out to make a case against me!"

He studied the sanctuary with its Victorian windows ablaze with colour. His Victorian childhood had left its mark. But his taste was more pre-Raphaelite than neo-Gothic. The tarot cards which he designed, and Freida Harris painted, would lend themselves very well to a treatment in stained-glass. "I swear," he went on, "I swear before the vast unknown that I have done no conscious hurt. I shock, I scoff, and I offend because I believe that is good for the smugness of the self-righteous soul."

He led me to a small door hidden behind the pulpit. "There is a great difference between evil and wickedness. You won't understand so, instead of explaining, I'm going to show you some very wicked people indeed."

Ghosts

We went down the narrow stone stairs and fumbled our way through the gloom. "Sorry, old son. They may be hours. But I daren't risk using a pocket-lamp in case the vanguard are on duty.'' He crouched down against the wall and then sat with a soft plop. "How about a quick lesson to help fill in the time?"

"My mam says cold stone can give you piles," I said.

"Your mam is right. I've got piles." He giggled softly.

"Your mother's wisdom aside, is there anything you'd like me to talk about?"

My eye were not yet adjusted to the gloom of the crypt but I felt cold and my skin prickled. "Ghosts," I said. "Tell me they don't exist."

"Telling lies won't help."

My head twisted round in shock. "You mean they do exist?" I remember every single thing he told me, he had my full attention, mind, so that I would not hear anything else. "Pagan religion," began Crowley, "smells more of cow-muck than sulphur! It says that Man is part of nature so he should try to build on this affinity... and stop being so damn proud of his own intelligence."

"In the twenties and thirties, the world became sceptic. The swing toward atheism is caused by man's admiration for his own achievements. It is the religion of technology. And what are the consequences? ... a mind anaesthetized, a false reality, and an environment that is too dense, too loud and too bright. We are not aware of anything other than our own sensations. The larger truth goes unheeded."

He paused and in the dark his hand encircled my shoulder. I don't know whether he was comforting me or measuring my reaction.

"Real people are not afraid of their dead," he went on. "They don't even feel separated from them." He nudged me gently. "Remember the time I took you to Brompton Oratory to hear the chanting?"

"Yes," I said. "you snorted too loudly."

"Only when they sang the 'Salve Regina' and got to the bit about 'in hac lachrymarum vale'! For God's sake, this world is not a Vale of Tears."

This was true. He totally despised the Christian obsession with death, dying, judgement and punishment or reward. "Why would the Gods treat men like sausages?" he demanded. He remembered the incident and grumbled under his breath. "Anyway," he said, "even though an actor walks off stage and sheds his body like a costume, the soul hasn't thereby ceased to be. Death is not an eternal goodbye. It is just the start of another stage of growth. From that moment on, the soul belongs by rights in 'that world there' — but it quite likes to keep in touch with its origins in 'this world here'."

He paused for a mere split second. It gave me the feeling he was touching on something crucial. "The dead can be heralds," he said. "They can bring and take messages. They can act like guide-dogs for the blind and bring a *Bright One* back."

"What's a Bright One?" I asked.

He seemed not to hear me. Or perhaps it was the wrong time to pose the question. I learned later that a Bright One is a benevolent spirit, filled with compassion, who tries to set man's handiwork to rights. It is not too far from the Buddhist concept of a Bodhisattva, except that a Bright One has not passed through a worldly existence. He has never lived among us.

The Dead

"A man is missed," Aleister went on, "by those whose lives crossed his. He is mourned by those who feel a void. But the weepers too will die. That is part of their sighs and sadness. They gather where their own graves will be dug, and grieve also for themselves."

"But at each farewell," he said, "there are fewer who remember the ones who have gone. Fallen fruit is soon replaced by new buds for life must go on. Familiar faces are weeded out and soon there is no remembrance. We are born into the present but tethered to the past, and there is a silver cord that pulls us on to the future. Survivors forget about this. They leave that cord to rot. And that is how the bond between the worlds is severed."

For Crowley, this bond was a two-way thing which the living should learn to use. The dead might choose to travel back but we had also a right to call them.

"Like gravestones scraped by the wind," he said, "souls lose their names. Then they take the path to a higher plane." It wasn't clear if this advance was a change of state, a blending of one's being with the gods, or reincarnation. It seemed all might be possible depending on a person's state of readiness i.e. has he the will to let go of identity. Our eyes had adapted to the dark, so when he looked round, I wondered what the hell he was seeing. No doubt he was watching for visitors, but my nerves were on edge.

"Some souls can't let go," he said. "Whatever the reason, they climb out of the train at the last minute and linger on the empty platform dismayed that everyone has gone. They wander the unknown streets like lost dogs. These are those amnesic ghosts who will gratefully follow anyone who happens by."

My heart pounded but worse was still to come.

"There are malignant souls too who break the rules, burst back through the barriers and outrage nature. They must hide from the Sweepers though — those who sift through the drains and snuffle in dustbins like jackals or blow-flies. These scavengers feed on living spirit, not on dead meat." "They must also hide from the Bright Ones, who would dispatch them to the darkness like criminals. What do they do then, these lost souls? They home-in on troubled minds. They squat inside people who are too harassed to notice the unbidden guest."

His sigh was so deep and so sincere, it sounded like a groan. "It is how the seeds of madness are sown." He looked at me sadly. "Modern medicine laughs at Jesus for casting out evil spirits, but they themselves are no nearer finding a cure! Mental illness is so widespread that hospitals are criminally overcrowded. Do you known what will happen? They'll invent a neater system of diagnosis and put thousands of sick people onto the streets to manage as best they can." He closed his eyes in anger and grief. "How mad are psychiatrists to ignore a method that works?" His resonance changed, going up a notch, as if he were shifting gear. I realised he was adopting his celebrated magic voice.

"In seventy years of life, we pass through seven stages. Seventy years after death, no one will remember us. In that world there we climb seven steps to yet another gateway. And we may quit this world by seven routes: mishap, malady, malice, neglect, age, suicide, and ousting. There are seven black keys and seven white ones. There are seven calls, seven questions, seven answers, seven deadly sins, seven holy virtues and seven Sleepers in Ephesus."

"Why are the seven stars no more than seven?" he howled like King Lear. "Because they are not eight! Ah, thou woulds't make a good fool, nuncle!" He glared at me as though in a seizure. "Do you know the line that should follow but was never committed to paper?" He stared into the distance as if seeing a vision. "And thou, fool, woulds't make a merry king!"

Tears trickled down his cheeks.

The Black Mass
He cocked his head slightly. "Not before time, I do believe they are coming at last." He drew me further back so we were better hidden in a corner. "In Borneo, I believe, they let corpses putrefy, put the bones in bags and hang them up in their long-huts. I can't see that catching on in pubs, eh?" He shook with mirth.

"Shh!" I hissed. "The gate is opening."

Between his teeth, Aleister sang a music hall ditty: "At Trinity church I met my doom..."

"They'll hear you," I hissed.

"Oh no," he assured me. "They are too far gone! To get their attention now, you'd have to fire a cannon — possibly that one!" He pointed at the priest but was very miffed when the old joke went completely over my head.

"I thought crypts were full of bones?" I asked.

"Yes. Nameless bones when the old graves are cleared to make room for new ones. In France they have a ceremony called The Second Burial. Villagers polish the bones before they're put in the crypt."

"But I've not seen any bones here," I insisted.

"They are under the floor, silly. That's why those poor idiots are stamping their feet: to insult the sacred memory of the dead."

The priest hoisted the choirboy's robes, who was as naked as a newly shorn sheep. Then flinging him on to a make-shift table in front of the altar, he dropped his own pants and proceeded to sodomize him. No, I was not so young that I didn't know about these things!

"I read somewhere that they were supposed to de-flower a virgin?" I said.

"Difficult to come by, these days. All that rationing, I'm afraid. You can only get them slightly sullied. But what does it matter anyway? If anything, society is even more sickened by the thought of sexual acts between men. Give credit where it's due: they're at least trying the second nastiest thing on the list."

I studied the scene with a critical eye. "But why doesn't the boy scream?" I asked.

"Because, dear heart, he very probably likes it." He gave an exaggerated sigh of mock patience. "If you'll open your eyes a bit wider, you'll notice that our choir-boy is wearing make-up. This could mean that they are making a film... but taking everything else into account, I think he wants to look a bit younger than he is. In addition to which, all else being equal, I suspect he's a young man who just likes wearing make-up."

This fascinated me because, as far as I knew, I'd never in my life seen a man with make-up. I couldn't judge though. I just had to take Aleister's word for it.

To be quite honest, the proceedings did seem a bit boring and tedious. Even the congregation, if that's the correct word for them, seemed not to be very involved. Nobody was holding his breath in suppressed excitement. One or two or them actually yawned. Even the 'victim', the boy plastered with Max Factor, looked as if he would like to whistle. Although the priest was sweating from the effort, he was clearly past his prime, and everyone looked set to be stoic about it.

It was just about as gripping as watching a lawn being mowed. Time passed, of course, as time will, and in due course it did rather seem as if the clergyman was — how can I put it — putting his foot on the pedal a bit. It could all have been an illusion of course, but it did sound as if the rhythmic battering of the boy's buttocks was speeding up a mite. Not to put too fine a point on it, the batsman's stroke was growing more powerful!

A wee bit too powerful, in fact, because the trestle at his end of the table became dislodged. Within a very few seconds his end of the table crashed to the stone floor with a clang and a loud scream from the crazed chorister. This left the parson at his end going purple as he was hit simultaneously by both the agony and the ecstasy! His yodel of anguished pleasure was drowned by an unearthly screech from the choirboy who was writhing on the paving-stones like a badly pecked worm.

"Dear me," hissed Crowley. "The poor sod's gone and trapped his knackers. That ought to summon something, don't you think... if only the fire brigade!"

I crammed my knuckles into my mouth and buried my face in my arm-pit.

"You should not laugh", said my father in mock disapproval.

"That poor boy doesn't find it funny."

My god, but I did though. I was shaking hysterically, as of course he had meant me to. I all but choked as I tried to stifle my laughter and Crowley wrapped his coat round my head.

But the worst was yet to come!

Rosemary's Baby

The assembly quickly restored some sort of order, and the next step in the ritual was a mock birth. Imitating the real movements and gestures of doctors and nurses, they pulled a lifelike doll from somewhere between the boy's legs. Now, while no one was injured as gravely as they felt, there was a certain amount of blood around. So when the new-born doll was held aloft, it looked so extremely credible that one woman swooned and another, the good neighbour no doubt, dropped into sympathetic labour pains.

The priest then baptised the baby in reverse, which means precisely what it says. He took a bucket in which all the men had relieved themselves, muttered the relevant words backward, and signed the doll's buttocks with inverted signs of the cross. What you might call being thorough. However, before I could stop him, Crowley let out a perfect imitation of a baby's cry at the precise moment when that sort of thing would be likely to occur in any normal baptism. The effect was riveting!

It was as if the sprockets had been stripped off the film and the scene simply froze. They were rooted to the ground. They did not dare to credit what their ears told them they had heard. The filter in the brain was clogged. They could not cope. They stood stock still, like tailors' dummies, as their feverish minds tried every known kind of logic in order to deny the evidence.

Suspiciously, cautiously, like lovers in a graveyard who suspect there is one hand too many, they slowly resumed their actions. Crowley squalled again.

Again they froze. But this time eyes were very much wider and eyebrows had lifted several inches higher. It was like a tableau at a waxworks museum except that every chest heaved and every heart pounded. The priest glared in horror at the doll. The choirboy gaped in disbelief at his genitals. The men and women of the congregation tried desperately to gaze into infinity so as not to see whatever there was to be seen. You could see their brains working. Once: it could be a false impression, a case of mistaking one thing for another. Twice: it could be a rat, a squeaky hinge, some slight escape of pneumatic pressure. Thrice would be unthinkable...

With exquisite timing, Crowley did it again. This time letting out the full, vexed cry of an infant that is close to the end of its tether. The priest's jaw dropped as if someone had cut the string. The choirboy was pawing at his perineum to see if, by chance, a birth canal had opened up. The ring of eyes belonging to the assembly lowered hesitantly to gawp at the central figures and to back away very softly.

To tell the truth, none of them looked like the epitome of evil. Who were they, when all was said and done? Just bored members of the local bourgeoisie — some more bored than others. They were dabblers, amateurs, wholly raw beginners. They had got together to try and whip up some thrills by being "ever so naughty". But they hadn't counted on this. They had not expected this. Now here they were — with growing evidence that their carryings-on had somehow thrown a spanner in the cosmic works — and brought about a prodigy! That was too much. The brain back-fired. The driver jumped out of the car. The pilot pulled the rip-cord. Each and every person seemed to change gear and jolt into a state of pure panic all at the same time.

The choirboy was the first to move. Fearing that his wildest dream had in fact come true, he kicked the slop bucket over the padre's trousers and fled. The sizeable crowd of onlookers melted away like the cartoon ghosts in the film Fantasia. The stricken priest tottered toward the exit, bouncing like a drunkard from one pillar to another, as he mumbled his first words of penitence for a very long time, and no doubt went upstairs to restore his odour of sanctity.

12
SEKHMET

The goddess of terrible war with the head of a lioness

Spoils of War
It wasn't easy, growing up during the War. It was selfish to complain while so many terrible things were going on, but if you're not there, you don't realize. All that sort of thing was just something we saw on the newsreels that were shown before the Big Film at the cinema. We knew about them. We cheered the good guys and booed the bad guys but as kids we weren't all that sure which was which. War was not real for a long time. It became real though when the bombs started falling on the industrial cities of the North.

Until then we were more concerned about the meagre sweet ration, the absolute tastelessness of school dinners, the baffles we had to buy for bicycle lamps — and that damn gas-mask we had to carry everywhere. If ever you lost it, your gas-mask that is, any cinema could fit you up with a new one. They collected hundreds that had been left on seats. We all found that very funny. It became the great tease of the year: "And what were you up to then that made you forget your gas-mask on the back seat?"

My uncle went into the army. Luckily for him, he was sent to India where he became a cook, and he never saw any fighting at all. Len Standish, my mother's husband, fared very much worse. He was caught in France and when the order came to evacuate Dunkirk. He was one of the several thousand to get badly hurt on the beaches. Even worse, when they got him on board a rescue ship, the bloody thing got bombed and he was terribly burned. We knew nothing at all about it at the time. The details came through two months later in an official letter marked War Office. Some officer or some clerk had copied out the standard phrases for such a thing. "We regret to inform you..." etc. The upshot was that Len Standish was undergoing "restorative surgery" at a special unit in East Grinstead, wherever that might be. They had not yet invented the term 'plastic surgery'.

I can't remember whether I was told about this or learned about it later. I don't think I would have understood anyway. Hospital didn't mean much. It was where they once took me when I had a nose-bleed. Besides which I had no deep feeling for this man. To put it bluntly, I did not love him at all. I just felt, intuitively, that he had some hold over me and I was terribly worried that he might decide to take me away one day. Apart from that, nothing.

Reality, when it came, hit me very hard. There was a knock on the door. I went to open it. There stood this thing, this plate of ox-tail soup with eyes. I could not speak. I couldn't even move.

"Is your Mam in?" the monster asked in a rasping voice. A pair of hands grabbed me and whisked me away upstairs. I sat near Grandma as she darned some socks. She said nothing. She showed no emotion at all. Just that hypnotic weaving of her needle, over and under, across the wooden mushroom. I tried not to shout but I was worred about leaving my Mam with that thing downstairs.

It was awful when she opened the stair-door and came to fetch me. "It's your Dad," she said. "He's been hurt in the war. It's not his fault that he looks... the way he does. I want you to be a good boy, a brave boy, and go for a walk with him."

He had insisted on his legal rights. It didn't matter what effect it might have on me — he wasn't going to let go. She could probably have persuaded the court to suspend things, but the truth was she felt sorry for him in spite of everything. She hadn't the heart to make him suffer any more. Even in their most violent quarrels, she had never once flung it in his face that I wasn't his son.

A Hero's Death

I was dumb-struck, of course. I had to go with him, but I felt so ashamed. His face was worse than Lon Chaney in 'The Phantom of the Opera' and I hated being seen with him. Other people's glances made me blush. I was on tenterhooks in case we passed any boys who knew me at school. A policeman saw the whiteness of my face. "Is this little boy with you, sir?" he asked. He checked my dad's papers and then gave him a proud salute. "I beg your pardon, sir. You must be proud of your father, eh lad?"

But I wasn't. I was hardly breathing. When he touched me, it almost hurt. When he kissed me goodbye, I had to freeze so as not to scream out loud. I never felt any pity. I never once thought how he must have felt... at least, not then. Not while I was a child. I just felt panic-stricken. My brain couldn't cope with what was happening to me. That is how I began the great lie of my life. If anyone asked, and they did ask, often, for my father's name and profession, I used to say "Dead. Soldier, killed at Dunkirk." Instead of the horror I expected, I got looks of sympathy, even admiration. I hadn't meant to be the son of a war hero, but that is what I became.

Naturally, the other kids questioned me closely and I had to pad the story out by supplying more detail. I invented madly. We were saving up so that one day we could visit his grave in France. My mother had been sent a *post hymn house* medal by the King. Little by little, the lie became a habit, and the habit a kind of second reality. Once launched, there was no way to stop it. It caused me trouble when I did my National Service because I had to write it all down on documents. They let it go. They let it drop because they probably thought that this was what I believed.

To do her credit, my mother didn't divorce him. It was his violence that was the problem — that and his jealousy. She was not going to do him any more harm than she already had. She did go through with it thirty years afterwards, but even then — only because she worried about any claims he might try to make if he got himself into debt. Len Standish died only some thirteen years ago and he never did find out that I wasn't his son.

I cannot judge what my mother did. She was poor and desperate, and Aleister never gave her any financial help "... in case it gave the show away..."! The fact that I was something of a cuckoo's egg never bothered me either and it didn't do Len much harm. I learned after that he was very proud of me. He used to boast about me to chums in the pub. They never believed him until I turned up for his furneral. That was the shock of their lives. But I still wish I'd never lied about him being killed at Dunkirk. He wasn't a hero. He didn't do anything special. But he never asked to be blown up and disfigured either, so I should not have diminished that.

I was sent back to him once. My mam developed a heart disease and they couldn't feed me without her wages. It was a nuisance for him but I felt trapped in a nightmare. There was a woman, Auntie Barbara, who understood my stress and was very kind. All he ever did was interrogate me over and over again about my mam. I think he was looking for some kind of revenge. "If she has a boy-friend, you know, you could come back and live with me." God knows why he thought this would be an inducement. As a matter of fact she never did remarry. She had her friends, of course, but I think one husband had been enough for her. She ran a little business and retired comfortably many years ago.

But while I stayed in Len's house I was so miserable that I wrote to Aleister Crowley off my own bat. My mam would have been furious if she had known. There would have been a catastrophe if my dad had found out. I couldn't help it though. Inside a week, I was back with my mam and grandmother. Debts had been settled and she received a postal draft from the army — "money which has been deducted from your husband's pay" was how they explained it. Evidently, Aleister had contacts in high places and could manage things quite cleverly.

Mum's the Word
There were witty posters on every wall as well as in buses and trains. They warned the public to be careful about what they said to others. "Watch out! There are spies about!" said one. "Careless talk can cost lives" said another. The most effective one of all just said: "Walls have ears!". It grew into a kind of paranoia. If you chatted away too gaily, someone in the next seat would tap you on the shoulder and point at the poster. You blushed as red as any guilty spy. This state of tension was made even worse by the fare we got from British films, most of which were to do with the effect of espionage. It wasn't 'public information' they were giving so much as something to take our minds off things. There were scores of costume dramas, I remember, and they all helped us to forget the joylessness of daily life and rationing. The government poured tons of money into the industry. They saw it as part of the campaign to neutralize enemy propaganda. Countless journalists, broadcasters and film-makers have spoken of it in their memoirs. If you want to get the flavour of it all, read Laurence Olivier's account of how his film 'Henry V' was made!

It may seem strange now, but every street name, signpost, and bus sign was expunged with black paint. Any inscription on stone that could give a hint about the town was filled in with plaster or boarded up. There was a Latin motto dating from the 17th century, that wound around the grammar school walls. Workmen filled it up with cement and painted over the lot. We schoolboys wondered how kraut soldiers could possibly read Latin and why they would want to locate our school!

If ever the dreaded invasion came, the Germans would not get any help. But while all these measures were designed to make it difficult for 'them', they also made it hard for us. Once you were off your home territory, so to speak, you were quite literally lost. It was no good asking any old passerby for a bit of help in finding your bearings. If you couldn't prove you were also British, you would soon be faced with a policeman or a squad of soldiers. In practice, of course, things worked more smoothly and more informally than that. In Huddersfield for example, they would ask you if you knew that town just before Marsden. On paper it is spelled Slaithewaite, but it is pronounced Slow-it, to rhyme with How's it. Or else you could mention a mill where your uncle worked, or give the date of the Holmfirth Flood — that little town on the edge of the moors that has since achieved fame through the television series 'Last of the Summer Wine'. Any one of these little shibboleths proved that you were "all reet". If you belonged, you could prove it. If you couldn't prove it then you didn't bloody-well belong, and that was that. It was all so much more sensible than Identity Cards which could be forged anyway.

We kids had a competition to see who could get himself arrested most often but the police told our Headmaster and he warned us that the next spy in short trousers would do fifty lines a day for the rest of the war. After that, there were fewer pint-sized paratroops asking for "zee Lorndorn train".

My young aunt was furious with the police when she had to come and rescue me once. "Common bleeding sense should tell you," she yelled. "A child that age is not capable of being a bastard spy!"

"I wouldn't put it past them," moaned the sergeant, "They have a Hitler Youth Movement, you know. They're like the boy-scouts, but ruthless with it."

"I'll tell you how to catch spies," my auntie confided. She was a mill-girl with all the richness of a mill-girl's vocabulary. "Lock up the shit-houses and put Epsom Salts in the streams! Then you could put nets out and catch them like bleeding flying-fish!"

Sea Shells

It was much more difficult now, going down South. Even to travel to London, you had to obtain special permission with a fistful of documents. To go further still — to the South coast for instance — you needed 'urgent family reasons' along with certified evidence. This is where my Grandad, and a cooperative local doctor, came in very useful. He was getting on in years and not too steady on his legs. He lived all alone and, quite naturally, needed to see his grandson. Not that I was his only grand-child — my young aunt had a daughter, and my uncle had a son — but none of them were being summoned by Aleister Crowley. When he wanted something, he usually managed to get it. Sometimes, the first thing we knew about a visit was the arrival by registered post of the official travel permit.

The worst aspect of wartime travel was the awkwardness of food-rationing. You could buy meals in restaurants and cafés, but if you stayed at a hotel overnight, the management required your ration book! Even if you went to stay with relatives or friends, it was tacitly understood that your ration-book came too. It was always declined the first time you proffered it, but if you didn't push it forward again, you got no meat, no butter, and saccharine tablets in place of sugar. Food was in short supply and, looking back, it's a wonder how we managed.

13
ANHUR

He who leads what has got away, the creative power of the sun, the one who found the eye

Leaflets
When I went to Aleister though, he told my Mam not to worry about such trivial things. She could keep the extra food for herself because he had lots of friends who were farmers. When you got to the station, most of the trains were reserved for troop movements. But I had a label tied round my neck, and many a friendly Tommy would lift me abroad. No need for me to hide behind kit-bags or have my ticket ready. There were very few stops and no inspector. If you used a civilian train though, there were still hordes of soliders. But they were not allowed to sit, even if the seats were empty. They bunked down in the corridors, or underneath the benches, and if you had to go to the toilet, you picked your way through a khaki beach and did your utmost not to tread on sleeping fingers.

My papers were examined by Army police, Civil police and even by men in plain clothes who didn't look like police at all. On one such trip, when the war was not going well, I had to get them out twenty-seven times! There was good reason for such heavy security. The South Coast was under relentless attack from enemy gun-fire. During daylight, you could see the tell-tale puffs of smoke. At night you could even see the flashes. All binoculars and telescopes had been confiscated. Only army or the Home Guard were allowed to study the French coastline. They kept look-out from a series of pill-boxes that stretched all along the cliffs. Wailing Winnie, or the siren, was reserved for air-raids only. So when shells were on their way, they gave a series of loud blasts on whistles. Other wardens would pick it up, one after the other. The sound spread outward like the shriek of eagles.

We ran for cover in total silence. Our ears strained to catch the sound of that other whistle — a shell flying through the wind toward us. It seemed as though the whole world had held its breath and then — whoompf — the explosion. Most of the time they came singly. But the Germans varied the pattern as if to keep us guessing and stretch our nerves to the maximum. They were trying to destroy morale at the lowest possible price.

Birds soon learned to stop singing when the whistles sounded. It was as though they knew that thunder was in the offing. Once they felt that strange drumbeat in the ground, they would start singing again. Once the "all-clear" sounded, we trooped to see what was gone and what remained. On bad days a barrage might last for an hour. Your head was split open just by the noise. It could damage your ear-drums of course, but it also drowned out the screams.

There was some kind of incident every day. It was to stop the Allies from mustering a fleet, said the most popular rumour. Others said it was to hide the fact that the Germans were getting ready to invade. Where do we run? we wondered. What do we do if the ships start coming? Stories were rife. They spread like wild fire, helped by the leaflets that enemy airplanes dropped just to mislead the public. The police told us to burn them or hand them in. I kept dozens and back at school, in Yorkshire, I sold them for sixpence each.

Foxy Lady

It's odd how trivial things stick in the memory. Once, when Aleister held a meeting at his house, I was fascinated by the men's winged collars — 'turned-up to Jesus', my mam called them. Another time, I was intrigued at the way women seemed to stab so casually at their heads with hat-pins! Was that why they hardly ever took their hats off — so much trouble, the danger, getting them fixed back on again? I counted four in just one hat!

Aleister stared in stern disbelief at one set of hat-pins that bore small figurines of Egyptian gods. "In the days when they burned heretics, what would the Inquisition have made of that lot, I wonder?" He gazed at the woman impishly. She gave a cold smile an drew him into a corner, where they were serving a drink called 'green goddess'.

Seeing I was alone, a slinky woman draped with a fox-fur slunk in my direction. "So," she said in a voice that oozed hostility, "this is the whelp of our darling Great Beast?" My father's voice seemed to come from nowhere, floating over the heads of the throng. "Whatch it, Thelma!"

She seemed not the least bit surprised at his having heard. "Your precious father has the ears of a fox!"

I felt hostile. I don't know why. "Better than wearing one round your neck, especially when it's dead."

She looked at me with a mocking sneer. "Nobody wears them while they're still alive, you little fool! And why are you looking at me like that? I only bought it, you know. I didn't actually kill it with my own bare hands!" She took hold of the fox's head and made a feint at my neck. But a ring got caught on one of its teeth, and her wrist seemed somehow to be seized in its gaping mouth.

"It bit me," she screamed, flinging it away from her. "The beastly thing is alive!" There was blood trickling down her arm.

"Come, come," smiled Aleister as he glided his way to her side. "You know as well as I do that such a thing is impossible. Besides which, if your husband bought it, it is probably only rabbit." He shot a glance with his eyebrows raised and got someone to take her to the bathroom.

Oh how I wish I could give more detail about the places where these things happened. But as I've told you, all signs had been obliterated, and to be frank, Crowley changed address quite often. I remember Hastings because of the famous battle, and I was very disappointed that the streets didn't bristle with arrows. I can also recall passing through a chain of small seaside resorts, as alike as peas in a pod. The houses gleamed with hygiene and pride. The streets shone with silver hair. We did make a special trip to Brighton and the Royal Pavilion was closed.

I have been back, of course. I have tried to jolt my memory by eating scampi and chips all along that part of Britain's coast. But I don't recognize these towns. It's like trying to remember the pantomime scenery after being dazzled by Cinderella! They are merely an anonymous backdrop. The name Sevenoaks stirred something in me — but it probably stuck simply because it struck me as odd back in those days. I know I once changed trains at Maidstone. I remember how someone laughed when I pronounced Lewes as Loos.

I don't doubt I could make up this kind of detail, if I were so minded. But where would it get us? There are gaps in my story simply because... there are gaps in my memory. That seems to be perfectly natural.

Canterbury

Aleister urged me to visit grandpa who was living near to Folkestone, you recall. I went by bus, and sometimes the husband of the family took us out on 'The Chocolate Round'. We went with a wagon loaded with empty oil-drums and did a tour of twenty or thirty outposts tucked away in fields, woods, and on the cliffs. We emptied the tubs that the soldiers used as toilets. With the floor creaking under the weight of the slopping drums, we would go to a field designated by the authorities and there we would empty the contents across the surface of a field. The War Office paid us, the farmer paid us, and I got a nice bit of pocket-money.

One day though, Aleister, grandad and I went in a car to Canterbury. It was very rare to get access to a car and we were stopped a few times along the country roads.

"Why are we going to Canterbury?" I asked Aleister.

"We can't be sure that the cathedral will survive," he said sadly. "There are a few things that I want you to see."

I remember it as if it was yesterday. As we walked along a narrow street, my grandad stopped by a shop that sold glasses. He jabbed a finger at one of the objects on display. It looked like a glass ball on a stem, with a rotor inside that turned endlessly.

"Let's see what schooling has done," the old man smirked wryly. "What makes yon thing turn all the time?"

The spinning vanes were black material one surface, white the other, and as I crouched to look for wires or whatever, my shadow fell across them and rotation stopped. I hid my grin of triumph as I turned round. "Sunlight," I pronounced airily.

"Clever bugger," snorted my grandad as he spat some tobacco juice into the gutter. But I didn't miss the proud wink that flashed between him and Crowley.

I had seen a big church at my sister's funeral but apart from that just a library and a railway station. Nothing had prepared me for the size of this cathedral. It was the space, the sheer space. It was so enormous that when you stood in the middle and looked toward the end, it almost seemed as if there were a mist. How amazed I was to stretch my neck and follow the pillars soaring upward like branching trees. How incredible was the colour of the paving-stones as the light from the stained-glass windows dappled them like the floor of an ancient forest.

"Very few people realise," Aleister said, "that these Gothic miracles were wrought by men who followed the old religion. I speak of the faith that was here before the arrival of the pope's men. These great centres of worship mark sites which have been sacred for thousands of years. Every stone, every image, is seamed with smoke and throbbing with ancient echoes." He caressed one of the pillars and our eyes followed it upward, all the way to the roof. "They held trees in very great reverence," he murmured. I understood at once. The fan-tracery represented real branches, and the colonnades were the arched avenues one finds running through forest glades. Everything was designed to draw eye and soul toward the altar, or the high place. For there was hidden a gateway that led to that other world.

"One could view Stonehenge as a nobler version of this," he said. "A circle of stone trees, simpler, but even more majestic in its own way."

Human Sacrifice

We went toward the shrine of Thomas à Becket. The history books at our school never called him a saint, but the ones at the Catholic school did. I knew the story well enough. I felt myself surrounded by the wash of history.

Once again, Crowley stood quietly and his voice was low and almost devout. "This man was one of the last, real druids! Can you imagine the scandal caused when the King showed how much he loved him? He showered him with favours. First he made him his chief minister, and then he made him Archbishop of Canterbury and Primate of All-England. And him a Saxon at a Norman Court."

"There were many earlier cases though. Saint Patrick once reported to the pope that he had ordained fifty druids in a single day and that he had considered four of them as bishops." My father looked at me as if willing me to understand. "Whatever it was that the church taught then — the gap between it and paganism was not very wide in those days!"

"Why did the King kill him?" I asked, thinking of the tragic story

I had learned at school.

"He didn't," came the reply. "Thomas was the double who died instead of the King. He offered himself as victim to replace his beloved friend." He regarded me with a pensive eye as he led me on. "There is another one over here."

"Another what?" I was so deeply moved by the story he weaved, my voice was all but a croak.

"Another of these strange, ritual deaths. Right up to this very day, he is known as the Black Prince." We gazed at the tomb with its stately effigy lying in eternal calm. "He too could deputize quite validly for the true king, his father. Under ancient bridges, in the foundations of old houses, we often find the bones of children. They were sacrificed in order to bring blessings on a man-made structure." He swept his hand out in a gesture that took in the cathedral and beyond. "In the great churches of Europe you will find these hallowed tombs. King William II, often known as Rufus, is to be found at Winchester. His grave in the choir is girdled by a series of funerary boxes containing the remains of Saxon Kings. At Worcester, of course, we have the tomb of King John."

He patted my shoulder as I stared at him agog. "You should never accept the state's own version of things, my boy. Whatever they say — teachers, vicars or bishops — there was an older religion that ran alongside the new one. Because it was diplomatic, England, France, and many other European countries were Christian — but only in name. Privately, outside the court, most of the monarchs still trod the ancient path."

It took us most of the morning to explore the great shrine. I saw that more of the windows were being stripped of their superb stained glass. Each fragment was being numbered, put in tissue and lodged in a crate. "In case o' bombs," said my grandad. "A bit late if you asks me."

"How it will change the mood," my father said. "With none of that incredible, rainbow glass, so much of the magic has also gone."

"There is no other way," I said in a bemused voice. "We must guard these places from wanton destruction because they too are sunlight machines."

Aleister regarded me a moment in stillness. Then he bent close toward the old man's ear. "You were right," he said in a stage whisper. "He is a clever bugger!"

"Makes me wonder where he gets it," sniffed my grandad.

14
ATUM

The bull-headed god, origin of the human race

Singing gongs
Aleister often spoke about the world of spirits and on a good day he would even spell things out, so that I understood them better. He had his own spirit taxonomy which included entities he called forms, but it was all too elusive for me. He even included animals but in a way that was closer to the shamanic concept of a visionary world rather than the Egyptian one. The souls of the dead were likewise included, although many of these had either decayed into something inferior and base, or developed into something higher and more noble. The final category was those ultra-beings which we ordinary humans think of as Secret Masters, Angels, Guides, or even Gods.

At the outset, this mish-mash of technical terms utterly bewildered me. It frustrated him enormously, but I couldn't make head or tail of it. It took a couple of years before they began to be familiar, and then the various components did indeed arrange themselves into a special kind of order which I could analyse.

"A bit like seeing 'The Cherry Orchard' or reading Tchekov in a book," he would say. "Don't be put off by all those Russian names. Change them! Call them what you want! It doesn't make a damn bit of difference. Whatever else, do not let your mind be blinded by an irrelevant detail which catches your eye only because of its oddness! Refuse to be baulked by it. Make it transparent. Go beyond! Then at least you will understand the story."

It was a helpful idea. It even worked with Tchekov's plays, I found. The older I grew, the easier it became to link things together and understand. But I have to admit that in the early stages, and especially the first time round, I got terribly confused.

It was like looking at the jumbled-up pieces of a jig-saw puzzle. I didn't know where to start.

He placed a great deal of emphasis on intuition and stressed that it was totally different from ordinary kinds of thought process. "When you have developed the strength of your own will, other people will have no need to ask you questions as you talk. If you try to think the way I will teach you, others will be able to drink in your word and find it more feasible to become Adepts."

When he touched on things of this sort, he did not sound at all like his normal, every day self. Somehow or other he changed. I couldn't yet tell whether he had been taken over by some higher entity or whether he was using the magick voice.

"Train your voice," he boomed, as if he'd been reading my thoughts. "Learn to speak the way I've described and no mere intellect will be able to resist or refute your arguments."

We had gone through a complete elocution course. I knew the 'Five P's' by heart: pitch, pace, power, pause and passion. That was not what he was on about. He was explaining to me that there was much more to pronouncing words than the techniques of breathing and acoustics. It was also to do with authority.

"Be heard on other planes," he said. "Be forceful. Cause other voices to compound with yours so that the resultant sound can be sculpted into power."

He made me practice by kneeling in front of a Tibetan gong which was shaped like an old aspidistra pot. It sat on a silk cushion and I sat about two feet away. He taught me to persuade the spirits of the gong to respond to the sounds I made so that sometimes, when I chanted, a strange music filled the air. That gong is still in my possession. I can still make it sing. Whenever I do that, other people's minds dance and their vision shimmers. The air itself seems to come alive.

Automatic Writing

One morning while we were eating breakfast, he said that he had business matters to discuss with a friend. I was to stay by myself in the library and write notes. "Not an essay," he insisted, "not a finished piece of work, but just the random thoughts that come into your head. Make no attempts to structure them or put them into any sort of order."

This sounded very much like one of those 'brain-storming'

sessions that managers do on business courses, or perhaps one of those 'free association' tests which psychologists were once so fond of.

"Your topic", he said, "is spirit. Scribble down as much as you can about spirit. Is there such a thing? Do we have spirit brothers? Is our own spirit double existing even now on some other plane? And while you're about it, ponder the suggestion that if we have spirit friends, we may also have spirit enemies! That there might be the equivalent of spirit police who might be chasing spirit criminals."

I was twelve at the time and when he sprang this sort of surprise on me, it felt worse than chemistry homework. Whatever way you look at it, he was asking rather a lot! There weren't even hints or guide-lines. The only other thing he said was "Get on with it!" There wasn't much point in saying it was all a bit beyond me. He could snort in several registers and wither your heart with one of his sideways glances, so it was out of the question to hand in a blank sheet of paper. He would explode with rage. He could take off like a rocket. He would let rip a diatribe on the meaning of words and ask me if I was as mindless as a mouse. I daren't risk it. I would have to try. So I sat down and wrote.

He read it through when we sat down to lunch. "Competent," he said and not much else. I was more than satisfied. It didn't sound much like praise, but it wasn't rejected either. I'd half expected him to toss it into the fire. He read it again more carefully. This time he gave a small chuckle or two and said he was pleased. This was harder to believe. Either he was teasing me or else he and his business associate had been hitting the bottle again. "Was it a good meeting?" I asked shyly.

"There was no meeting," he replied smugly. "I made that up so that you wouldn't ask questions. All the time that you've been writing, I was in the next room imploring the spirits to give you a helping hand."

"Good grief," I gasped, "was it all that important?"
"It was important that you did not know what I was up to!"

He scanned my scribble again. Here and there, his eyebrows lifted, and from time to time he gave a contented sigh. When he had finished, he gazed at me with pride.

"It is hard to credit, I dare say, but what we have here, young man, is the makings of something very significant indeed." He stuck out his bottom lip and looked at me like an antique dealer wondering how much to bid. "I propose that we join forces and turn this into a book. What do you say?"

The idea just left me breathless. "Am I good enough?" was all I managed to say.

"Never ask that," he snapped sternly. "Such a question ought never to enter your head. Of course you are good enough: you are my son!"

Our Joint Work

His words were not quite as arrogant as they sound. Aleister Crowley believed in the principal: we are not what we think we are, we are what we think! He saw at once that he had put the wind up me. "You look like a tortoise who is in two minds about whether to pull its head back in its shell," he said. "I wasn't pulling your leg, you know. I'm quite serious about our writing a book together." He stood up and paced round the dining-room table. "I always begin with the title," he admitted with a laugh. "Getting a good title is half the problem solved. What would you like to call your book? Any ideas at all?"

I shook my head, not really thinking about it at all.

"'Codes and Ciphers'?" he suggested airily. "Or: 'Trapdoors and Secret Passages'? If I remember my own childhood, that's the sort of thing that boys of your age like, isn't it?"

I nodded with a slight smile. "'Treasure Island', except it has already been used."

"Yes, yes," he grinned, ruffling my hair again. "Something exciting and adventurous. But this book..." he waived his hand in the air, "... This book is more serious than that. It's not just for children but for grown-up people as well. Mind you," he laughed loudly, "I did exactly the same thing at your age. I wrote terrible stories in school exercise books and loaned them out for a ha'penny a time." He smiled at the fond memory. "But the kind of title we need here is someting arresting, something that will catch the eye, capture the interest and intrigue the brain. Something with a purple light and a faint whiff of sulphur!" He tapped his chin with a fork and gazed into space. "I've got it," he snapped like the crack of a gun. "'Liber Fulgur'!

"'Liber Vulgar'?" I echoed.

"'Liber Fulgur'," he repeated, punching every vowel and every consonant.

This was more than I could cope with. "What?" I asked in a dazed voice.

"You do Latin, don't you? Then come on, you twerp. *Liber* book and *Fulgur* lightning. *Liber Fulgur*... "The Book of Lightning'!".

"But why lightning?" I asked. "It's got nothing to do with what I've written."

"It will have before we are finished!"

He clutched my few sheets of paper againts his chest as if they were a weighty treatise, and his eyes danced merrily as he rumbled with distant laughter. Then he was off again. A different look crept into his eyes as softly as a cat's nictitating membrane. His voice seemed to slip sideways. "This will be no ordinary book — no bundle of nice songs and cosy bedtime stories. They needn't look here for their reassuring, mental fairy tales! As for all those pious dreamers — with their fluffy, pink religion — this will give them bloody nightmares!" He thumped the table-top and made the spoon jump out of the salt cellar.

"Why lightning, you ask. Why lightning of all things? I'll tell you why." He began to shake like a man with fever.

"Because it will be both a revelation and a step toward the end. Because it will both quicken and kill. Greak oaks will fall and whole forests will be set ablaze!" His voice began to climb and swell and grow in a booming resonance. "Cowards will tremble like children under the sheets! But heroes will brandish their lances and the heavens to capture the power that will transmute them into *burning ones*. Men who are afire and can be seen across eternity."

He stopped dead, slightly breathless. A change came over him and he relaxed. He turned toward me and gave me a huge, Laurel and Hardy wink.

"In short," he said, "it will be rather a good book!"

Pink Religion

When Aleister used the expression 'fluffy pink religion', he was referring to the creeds and systems of belief which men bodge together out of nothing. He meant religions which have been invented purely for private comfort and have nothing at all to do with the truth.

"Scared shitless of life and paralysed by the thought of death," he said, all but singing Ol' Man River. "And in between, they are too bloody timid even to taste the truth! Is this thing the King of Creation? This wey-faced, lily-livered, green-gutless fool? King? A bloody clown, more like! King? More of a freak!" He had worked himself up into a fury now and was spluttering with rage. "Can we call this a Hero when it is frozen with fear by every damn thing it meets! What's his answer, this thin tallow dip? What's his solution, eh? He just re-shapes the cosmos, that's all. He paints it more to his own liking. He even revises Holy Writ so that it matches his opinions. As for God — he gives God the face that he sees in his own passport and that makes him feel such great chums!"

He pounded his temples in mock despair and pretended to pull out handfuls of hair, even though he had none. "What must we look like to the world beyond? What kind of spectacle do we represent on the astral plane?" His hands dropped in dismay. "Are these men, the gods will ask, or are they mewling babies?"

He went on like this for some time. He did something similar, off and on, all the years I knew him. I was his way of unburdenining his heart, I suppose. At any rate, we did eventually write our special book. To be more precise, I wrote it to his instructions, then he took it to bed and hacked at it with a fountain-pen, and I would make a fresh copy the next day. He altered words, changed phrases, cut and pasted whole sentences. When he had finished with it, I could scarcely recognize any of my original work.

"It's not your fault," he soothed when he saw my forlorn face. "We can't expect the moon at your age. Your command of words is too weak, your fluency is too slow, your horizons are still too narrow." None of this soothed my ego in the slightest. When the final version was finished, he tried to smooth things over by praising it to high heaven. "The potential was already there or I couldn't have done a thing. It was your material which inspired me to lend a hand. So I know more words than you — that only means I've translated; it does not mean I've re-written it. This is your work and the occult world will honour it as your apprentice piece. The diamond is yours — I merely cut and polished it."

He was laying the praise on a bit too thick! Even then, I knew enough to be suspicious. I took the book back to Yorkshire with me, and kept it in the bottom of the wardrobe, wrapped in brown paper. I've kept it, of course. Each time I've moved house, I have come across it and given it a dust down. I don't think I dare throw it away, but I daren't look at it again, either. It has just got dry and dusty for half a century.

It's more of a keepsake really. He did actually say that it was one of the proofs that led finally to my initiation. But more of that later.

15
SESHESTA

The goddess of writing and history, inventor of letters, mistress of the house of books

The Queen of Sheba

The Koran salutes the four faiths as being loyal to the one, true God: Judaism, Christianity, Islam and Sabaism. For no good reason, as far as I can see, people assume that the synagogue is the birthplace of both the Church and the Mosque. They overlook that fourth religion: Sabaism, or seem never to have heard of it. This is a very significant point though. It is a great deal to do with Aleister Crowley's concept of truth.

Like an old cardigan that one no longer has use for, the threads of that older religion, Sabaism, were unpicked and woven into the very texture of the three others.[1] The traces are clearly discernible if you look closely enough. You can actually see where the one set of beliefs has been patched or overlaid with another. It is like a copper bucket that has been mended with tin, or a temple veil whose tears have been repaired with a different colour of thread. We can still feel the touch of that older religion today. Its ideas and precepts have had a significant effect on history, and how we developed. It sleeps still in each man's unconscious memory. He would find it, if he knew where to look.

Sabaism was once very common throughout the whole of that area we now call Arabia but it seems to have been strongest in the region we call the Yemen. The followers of Sabaism felt that the 'source of all' could best be represented as the stars in the firmanent and all that lay beyond. They called this infinity the sabbaoth, and the Ultimate Being who resides in the vast and mystic *all* was known simply as 'The Lord God of Sabbaoth'. It

---

1. cf Manly P. Hall, *Secret Teachings of All Ages,* H. Crocker, 1928.

rings a bell, doesn't it? That is because the other religions adopted the title too. You have seen it in many a Christian church, painted in glorious scroll-work above the altar perhaps, or over the entrance to the sanctuary.

Crowley believed that Sabaism was the senior religion and the parent from which all the others were descended. It was already old and renowned when the Queen of Sheba, or Saba, paid an official state visit to King Solomon. Her name is given as Belkis of Balkis which means: 'she who is white'. But this is not quite as straightforward as it looks. Today we sometimes give a girl the name 'Blanche' in a way that means 'pure' or 'virginal'. In the Queen of Sheba's case it carried a slightly different meaning: "she who is white in spite of being black". Belkis is a very, very dark-skinned lady. This may have been why she was chosen to be Queen. The people of Israel put on a magnificent reception for the visit of this queen because, in coming to them in state, she was giving her endorsement to their growing political importance in the middle eastern world. The scribes considered it so extremely important that they even found space for it in both the Bible and the Koran.[2]

Like the Pharaoh of Egypt, the Queen of Sheba was more than a monarch, more than the hierarch of her country's religion: she was the living embodiment of the God. She was the divinity made flesh. Few of us today can imagine the impact that her presence had, or what significance was attached to it. The closest we can get is some people's reverence for the Pope — but magnified a thousand times. The lady was not just a Queen or a religious dignitary. The Sabbaoth was in her. Her person was holy.

Rastafarians

Solomon and the Queen of Sheba got on very well together. It is impossible to say whether either one of them set out to seduce the other, or even whether it was true love or a question of political expedience, as between Caesar and Cleopatra later on. At all events they became lovers, and she stayed with Solomon long enough to bear him a son. She was not condemned for this. The King's behaviour was not criticised. The child was given the

---

2. *The Holy Bible*: 1 Kings, Chapter 10, verses 1 to 13; Also *The Holy Quran* (sura 27, 30-31,45).

name Menelek because, in contrast to her, he was very fair-skinned, like his father. In the strange logic of magical language, Menelek means 'dark one' and his descendants founded the royal dynasty of the land we now call Abyssinia.

Before the civil war when the communists toppled the monarchy, the king's proudest title was an ancient tradition: The Lion of Judah. Before becoming king he was known as Ras (or prince) Tafari. The Rastafarian sect has its origin in The Universal Negro Improvement Association which was formed by Marcus Mosiah Garvey in Jamaica during the 1920's. When Ras Tafari was crowned as Haile Selassie, Emperor of Ethiopia, in 1930, the negro movement was filled with jubilation because a black man was an emperor. Marcus Garvey's main aim had been to persuade his fellows to go back to their homeland in Africa. He had prophesied that when a black King would be crowned, he would summon all black people home. My father and I met Marcus Garvey in Brixton, a few months before he died in 1940. He has not been totally forgotten. His name had been on people's lips from the day of Haile Selassie's accession to the throne of Ethiopia. The negro people of England, America and West Indies were enormously impressed by two of the special titles that were used during the enthronement ceremony: "King of Kings" and "Lord of Lords". Apart from being used in the Hallelujah Chorus from Handel's "Messiah", they are cited in the New Testament as emblems that will mark his robe and his thigh.[3] There is more in this than we realize because, quite clearly, the Rasta-men are doing something more than just boosting morale in the black ghetto.

I mention these things now because they helped me to get hold of the things I am going to describe next. I can't really claim that I understood them, not in the sense that perceived the underlying principals or got to the heart of the matter. No, I failed quite badly on that score. It has been harder to express myself here that at any other point in my book so the ideas I have raised just now are meant as a sort of mental scaffolding. At all events, they helped to give me a starting point, somewhere that I could begin to understand what follows. If you can't get it either, then do what I did and put it in a pending file.

---

3. *Revelations* 19, 16.

Caesar

"I want you to do some more automatic writing," he said one day.

Automatic writing is a strange phenomenon and looked at with a certain amount of suspicion in occult circles. The medium holds a pencil or pen, just as normal, but then cuts loose his mind. The idea is to detach his thoughts from his personal, everyday life and problems so that some other entity takes over his vacant mind, so to speak. Then he just controls the medium's hand to make it write. In theory, it isn't the medium who does the writing but this "something other". You can see why so many people are chary though: the whole process is wide open to trickery. When it is all boiled down, the only way one can judge the genuineness of this or that medium is by weighing the stuff that he writes. When Crowley suggested I try it again, my heart sank into my stomach, "Aw... Dad...!"

"This time you can do it while I'm talking."

Well, this was a bit more interesting. "Pencil or pen?" I asked cheekily, but before he could stab me with one of his glances, he shoved his 'Onoto' between my fingers. It had no nib but just a slender tube with a fine wire sticking out. In those days it was very posh. The latest thing. Nowadays these things are very common drawing tools in architects offices and so on. As gadgets go, this one was far too flimsy for a curious boy and I ended up breaking it. Aleister lay on the sofa, one hand behind his head, the other conducting an invisible orchestra. He took a few minutes to get settled down. He said nothing for a long time. He wasn't being dramatic at all. He was trying to find the right place to begin. I groaned inwardly. It looked like it was going to be a long day.

"When Julius Caesar burnt down a quarter of Alexandria," he began, "he was just trying to stop a kind of pincer movement by the Egyptian troops. Unfortunately, the wind shifted and took the flames in an unexpected direction. Purely by accident, he destroyed the greatest library in the ancient world." He picked his teeth a moment with a curious object made of ivory. "Very few books were saved from the blaze." He made a dramatic pause. "But I have one of them!" He never lied. On the other hand, his words didn't always mean what he seemed to be saying. It was something one had to get used to. You could never take what he said quite at face value. He wasn't cheating you or having a joke. He just used language differently. "Where did you get it," I asked, treading carefully.

"In Egypt, of course. When one is a Master, being handsome is less relevant than holding a magic wand, and nice things do occasionally happen."

Aiwass

When I think of Crowley's reputation, I smile to remember how embarrassed he was to touch on certain topics. He didn't seem to know how far he dare go or what quantity of news I could cope with. Not much of it was news at all. I was reasonably well-on in to adolescence by now. Not that it made much difference. Why is it that parents forget how young they were themselves when all the fuss started? Aleister would bend over backward to avoid certain topics.

"We were on a sort of holiday," he explained. He didn't give me time to ask who this "we" might be. "We were visited by a spirit being who said that his name was Aiwass and he, er, acted as our guide." He coughed. "Among many other things, he took me to meet a Beautiful Black Lady." He pronounced the last three words as if they were a title. "She told me where the book was hidden and how it had once been guarded by the Knights Templar for many years. Even then it was old beyond belief. It was ancient before it was rescued from the fire at Alexandria."

I imagined a bundle of newspapers tied together with a string, or something equally shambolic. Once again he showed that he could read my thoughts.

"It was nothing to do with what we'd think of as a book today," he went on. "It was a series of about a dozen scrolls. The biggest was about as fat as a drain-pipe, and the others were of all kinds of sizes. It appeared that they were numbered by means of knotted leather thongs, while their contents were indicated by coloured beads threaded between the knots. Evidently, there was some underlying principle like the Dewey System of modern libraries. But we never found what it was and I've never read about anything similar."

"The vellum had been specially treated to help preserve it as long as possible. Sadly however the stuff had been slowly rotting for years and by the time it reached me, the edges of the rolls were eaten away and whole sections had already crumbled into flakes and dust. We copied everything down, word for word, symbol for symbol." At that he fell silent for moment.

Of course, I can't say what the language was. He didn't tell me and it never crossed my mind to ask. I don't even know how it was written down — in hieroglyph, demotic, ideographs, or alphabet. I wouldn't have understood, and I wouldn't have remembered. Whenever I have thought about it since, and I do think about it often, my guess is some sort of syllabic writing. This is why Crowley referred to words and symbols alike.

"Sometimes though, the rolls would crack as I touched them. One heard the noise — like thin ice on a frosty morning. When that happened we were faced with the tedious task of putting the fragments together again and we spent the rest of the day lifting flimsy morsels with eye-brow tweezers. Since we were working in our hotel room, we shut all the windows to stop any breeze, and we hung the place with wet sheets to raise the level of humidity. What with one thing and another, it was quite hellish."

He came out now in a fine sweat as if he was living through it again. "The hotel staff thought we might have been touched my the sun and kept tapping at the door to see if we were all right. A couple of French guests were so nosey, they sent round an Egyptian doctor in case we'd both gone mad. God alone knows how they thought an Egyptian doctor would tell!"

The Sacred Book

He fell silent now as though watching a film that absorbed him. I hardly dared do it, but I had to give him a prompt. "What then?" I asked, softly.

His eyes turned to me and there was a look of genuine awe in them. "We were driven to keep going. Aiwass pressed us. It wasn't that we lacked the will or interest — it was the damn fatigue. 'Look how much we've done,' I would say. 'Look how little is left,' my friend would reply. And that was what kept us at it — the rolls getting fewer, the heap of frass growing as if we were beetles nibbling away the temple roof."

He slid his arm round my shoulders and now there was a slight catch in his voice, just like my mother when she described 'Gone With the Wind'.

"It held together just long enough." He went to the shelf and brought a huge book. "Is that 'Liber Legis'" I asked in a hushed voice.

"No," he said simply. "It is 'The Book of Desolation'."

He gave me that one and only copy to keep safe. It was not the original transcription though. It was his own rendition of the text in English. He had made it with the help of the spirit-being, Aiwass. I have read it, of course, and there isn't a great deal I can tell you. There are some typical Crowley touches, here and there, but on the whole it doesn't read like anything else he composed.

"But I thought that was the time you produced 'Liber Legis'?" I said in puzzlement.

"'Liber Legis' was written because I had to produce something," he said bitterly. "Certain people had got wind of bits and pieces of the story. I did 'Liber Legis' to put them off the scent." He shrugged regretfully. "Just a red herring, really."

"You mean there's no truth in it? You just made it up?" He smiled sadly. "Not as simple as that. I threw in just enough truth to make the cake taste of chocolate. Otherwise it is a work of my own invention. Not without merit though." But by this time I realized just how much value his followers placed on 'Liber Legis', and he could see that I was shocked. "It wasn't a question of cheating, old son. In many ways I may be a rogue, but not to that extent. I did what I did for very good reasons. There was the problem of the missing pages, you see. The text had gaps in it. Every scroll was damaged in one or more places. This meant that the book was flawed and left the way open for forgery and fraud."

He looked at me with eyes that were heavy and suddenly careworn. "One day you will tell them. They will not be able to criticise me. I did what I did under instructions."

A Missing Page

He reached across to a side-table and picked up a large, heavy volume. "What does that look like?" he asked, placing the book in front of me.

"I don't know. Perhaps an old photograph album?"

"It's a Bible, you dunderhead." He bowed his head and forced himself to speak more calmly. "I disguised the thing as a Family Bible of the nineteenth century. Surely, you've seen one of these before?"

"In church," I answered honestly. "The big book on the back of the brass eagle." I heard him suck his tongue in irritation. "The one we've got at home is only very small," I assured him hastily.

"My Mam won it for good attendance at Sunday School."

"It doesn't matter," he said with a patient sigh. "It doesn't have to be a bible at all. It could be a stamp album, one volume of an encylopaedia, or even a copy of the Beano Bumper Story Book for Boys." He gazed at me with hard, brilliant eyes. "The point is this: nobody will see its true form unless they have the special key."

He recovered his good humour and patted my back jokingly. "It would probably be as well to change it into something else. Who knows? Even bibles might be worth stealing one day."

How right he was! The book is now disguised as something else. I would be daft to say what, so I'm not even admitting that it looks like a book any more. My whereabouts are not widely known, and I have learned to be fairly secretive. You have to be when you are Aleister Crowley's son! If burglars came to my house, I don't think they'd even know what they'd stumbled up on. It doesn't look like anything of interest and you'd be hard put to it to guess it had any value. When Aleister first put it into my hands, I was a bit over-awed. I don't think I had really taken it all in, so it wasn't the historical or magical importance that impressed me. Believe it or not, I was fascinated by the intricate pattern of the carved wooden covers. It had brass hinges, and a special fastener such as you see on a jewel-box. "A pity that your original story isn't true. What I mean is — if Aiwass had dictated this, then there wouldn't have been any bits missing, eh? He'd have done the job properly and the book would be complete."

"Oh my dear, trusting boy! We dare not tell the truth. A book that was written by Aleister Crowley and on sale at many bookshops — that wasn't going to tempt anybody. But "The Book of Desolation', imperfect and incomplete, would have attracted rogues from every corner of the earth. Somehow or other, they would have tried to steal it."

"Well, it's still a shame," I grumbled. "Now we'll never know what the scrolls contained."

"Ah," my father replied, tilting his head to one side. "Never is rather a strong word." Then rather oddly, he held out his hands over my head and muttered something under his breath. "Do you believe," he asked, "the higher powers watch over and help us? Do you truly believe that?"

"Yes. I truly believe that."

"And so you should!"

His voice broke. He fell to his knees in front of me and waved my sheet of scribble in front of my face. "Otherwise... how it is possible that you, my young scallywag, have just written one of the missing pages?"

He squeezed me against him with gorilla-like strength and there was a strange scent of violets in the room.

"The Beautiful Black Lady is going to take very great care of you."

16
HOR-MERTI

He of the two eyes, the god Horus whose sun and moon see and search

MI5

Early in 1940, a few months after the war had begun, a group of strange men came to see Crowley. One was small, one was tall, and the other was rather fat. "With a harp and a cigar, they'd have the makings of a good comedy team," said Aleister when they'd gone.

The fat man spoke first.

"Mr. Crowley, you must have heard of me. My name is Louis de Wohl, the astrologer."

"No," said Crowley never loth to prick anyone's balloon. "I'm afraid it rings no bells."

The other flicked a glassy eye, a bit like Erich von Stroheim. One almost expected him to slap Aleister's face with a gauntlet. "These gentlemen are from a certain ministry."

"I thought they were air-raid wardens." He looked at the other two with a pleasant smile. "Good evening, gentlemen. Are my black-out curtains at fault again?"

Louis de Wohl bit his cheeks. "They would like you to help your country with the war effort. I too have been recruited."

"Perhaps you needed work," said Crowley acidly. "I'm glad to say that my own circumstances are quite secure." This was far from true. His finances were never secure. "In any case, you are Hungarian, if I'm not mistaken?"

"So you do know about me!" beamed the other.

"Not at all," said Aleister. "It's the accent. Puts me in mind of a bad actor in that thing by George Bernard Shaw — 'Pygmalion'. Do you know it?"

Mr de Wohl had the clear impression he had just been insulted but couldn't quite see how it had been done. He just drew himself up and let himself down again. "Whatever my nationality, I have given my allegiance to your government."

"And I'm sure my government is grateful. But it doesn't quite explain where I come in." He turned toward the others. "I'm sixty-four years old, gentlemen. I wouldn't know a rifle from a shooting-stick!"

"You would if you sat on it!" grinned the smaller man. The other gave him a nudge that must have bruised his ribs. "It is not a question of your becoming a soldier," he said in an oily voice. "But you do have other, more interesting qualities."

"I make a passable pot of tea," agreed Aleister. "Otherwise I am merely a poet, a pornographer, and the greatest living magician this century."

"You are also an expert on occultism," smiled the tall man. "On German occultism," the small one added with a smirk. "My colleague refers to the links between the Order of the Golden Dawn and certain German societies." The tall man watched Aleister closely. "One knows all about the Sprengler papers: the famous hand-written cipher document that had such an influence on the innder teachings of The Order of the Golden Dawn."

"It has long since been agreed that those papers were a forgery," snapped my father.

"Certainly," agreed the other. "But a forgery planted for a special purpose by close friends of the Kaiser! It is called long-term planning, Mr. Crowley. As was the visit you received in 1912 from Herr Theodor Reuss. He made you Head of the O.T.O. in England, I believe? But not an autonomous group, eh, Mr. Crowley? Subject, in fact, to instructions from headquarters... er... in Nuremberg, if I'm not mistaken." He smiled disarmingly but, as Aleister agreed later, he had done his homework.

Pressures

"Obviously," the other went on, "the intention had been to involve the sons of good families, even of statesmen. Men who might one day rise to high office. If, at the same time, they had also risen in the ranks of a secret society which had links with Germany...? No need to dot the i's or cross the t's, eh?"

Aleister looked at him as if he were an acute case of something incurable. "You tell it with all the gusto of another John Buchan.

That can only mean you are members of the secret service."

"And the service has a long memory, Mr. Crowley." The short man slapped a document on the table. "That is a copy of a pro-German article you wrote for the magazine: 'The Fatherland'!"

"Can I keep it?" asked Aleister. "I long since lost my own." If looks could kill, my father would have died on the spot. "It gives me no pleasure, Mr. Crowley — no pleasure at all — to speak to someone who once wrote propaganda for the enemy of his mother country!"

"Then you have a very small mind — for an Intelligence Officer! If only you had dug a little deeper, you would have found that I kept the British Government informed. Moreover, what I wrote was so blatantly extravagant, only a German would have believed it. Anyone else would have seen it for what it was: pure mockery! They paid me quite good money though. Because of that, the British Government decided to pay me less. Briefly, sir, I was acting under instructions."[1] He opened the door, inviting them to go. "You are not only uninformed, but rude and clumsy with it. Please be careful going down the steps in the dark."

The small man was seething with indignation. "Are you actually trying to tell us that you are a red-blooded, British patriot? You did what you did for money?!"

"Whereas you, I presume, do it for charity?" Crowley sneered at him with contempt. "Every labourer is worth his hire! When you get back to your kennels, have another look through my dossier. My last cheque arrived only three years ago. It was for work I did in Berlin!"[2] The other was staggered. "You know Berlin, do you? Very few toilets, you know! Almost makes one feel unwelcome."

The taller of the two was the first to recover his composure. "All that is water under the bridge," he said lamely, "and we haven't come here just to rake over old coals." He attempted a cheery smile but Crowley's face was still like a piece of frozen dough. The man cleared his throat nervously. "Before we can go any further though, I must ask you to sign this." He slipped a document across the table.

---

1. Aleister Crowley, *The Confessions*, Mandrake Press, 1929.
2. Michael Howard, *The Occult Conspiracy*, Rider, 1989.

"And what is it?" Crowley did not deign to look.

"A copy of The Act. That is to say: The Official Secrets Act. Anyone who works for the government is required to sign."

"I do not work for the government."

"You have just this moment admitted you were paid by them."

"Piecework, my boy. Not commissioned but cash on delivery. I believe you call it freelance."

The tall man sighed. "Nevertheless, you must sign this! It gives us a legal hold on you. If ever you say anything you shouldn't, you would be committing a very grave offence and — you'd be for the high-jump! In wartime, it would be classified as treason. And that, believe it or not, is still punishable by death in the Tower of London!"

"To mix my blood with that of Anne Boleyn — fame at last!" My father smiled wickedly. "Your offer is tempting but... I'm afraid I must decline."

"You have not heard our offer."

"Then pray, do tell me about it."

"That is not allowed, unless you sign."

Aleister blinked and raised his shoulders. "Then we can only declare it a stalemate. Unless of course you would care to forge my signature?"

The men from the secret service knew they were cornered. They had thought it was going to be easy since no one had told them how unyielding Crowley could be. "Please be reasonable," the tall man tried again. "It wouldn't be in anyone's interest if we had to force you."

"Force?" Aleister's face lit up. "Youse gonna give me da toid degree?" he asked in a phoney Bronx accent. "We had degrees in the Golden Dawn, you see, so I've always wondered what the films meant by that." He rubbed his hands gleefully and glanced around the room. "Is there anywhere special you want me to sit? Near to a naked light bulb perhaps?" He practically danced in his excitement but then, quite suddenly, he stopped and stared at them. "I have forces of my own, by the way. Powers and elemental beings put at my disposal. But any damage they do..." he did a little jig, "you are perfecly welcome to publish. Provided you survive."

The small man was all for having a go. The tall man just ground his teeth in fury and frustration. "If physical force would do the trick, I'd be the first to volunteer. I would so dearly love to call your bluff."

Crowley stopped dead in his tracks. "Then please call it, Major Lewis." The man jerked in shock at this use of his name. "You have come here uninvited, you have been bloody offensive to me under my own roof, and you suggested using force! I am master here, Major Lewis. The rules are mine and you have already broken them. Do please feel free to hit me. I give you your solemn word that I should not strike back. There would be no need." He glared at the man icily. "I challenge you, Major Lewis. I dare you, Major Lewis. Go right ahead and call my bluff."

Telepathy

It was quite obvious that the Major was not yet cowed. He simply saw Crowley as a pompous eccentric. His breeding compelled him to stay calm. His natural reaction was to try and humour the silly old fool. "Come along, dear chap," he said in his best Regimental voice. "You know what I mean. Your age and all that!"

Crowley's eyebrows shot up. "You mean your darling lady-wife, Felicity, would not approve? You think your two children, Doreen and Tom, would be ashamed? What about that touch of damp rot in your new house at Kingston?"

The Major was now going rather pale, changing from irritated red to a putty-coloured grey. "How...?" he gasped. "How do you know about them?"

"How do I know about the touch of damp-rot under the bathroom? How do I know about the immemorial elm that leans so dangerously across your smart new garage?" He bent in closer so that only the Major would hear. "How do I know about your little problem in bed?" The poor man's eyes bulged. "You have tried everything, no doubt, but I could help you very quickly in that department. And all without signing The Act!"

None of the others had heard the last remarks, but they could see the effect it was having on their colleague. He was bewildered, utterly out of his depth, and his training had not prepared him for it. He scrabbled around his mind desperately, searching for some instruction, some paragraph of instructions. He did what they'd done in the drama club whenever an actor forgot his lines. He carried on as if nothing had happened. He ignored all the red lights and alarm signals.

"If you would kindly sign the paper, Mr. Crowley, we could then discuss your terms of service. You would be suitably recompensed, naturally."

The menace was gone. Chaos had been in the offing but now, unexpectedly, it was tranquil. "You begin to make it sound more interesting," answered Crowley. "To take the chill off things could you just say what you mean by 'suitably recompensed'? Not that it has any direct influence on my decision."

The Major was uncomfortable when talking about money. He'd been taught at his old school that gentlemen just did not do this. "The salary of a Senior Technial Officer has been suggested along with one or two special allowances for use of car, dislocation and so on."

Crowley eye him suspiciously and hacked his way to the heart of the matter. "How much?" he asked bluntly.

"Two or three thousand. It can be haggled about."

"It will be haggled about," smiled by father. "I'm rather good at it. Quite essential in Egypt!"

He held out his hand for a pen and then did one of his slow, grand signatures in which the capital letter 'A' bore a shocking resemblance to the male sex-organs. The Major looked at it with no crack in his composure and handed it to his assistant. He then slid a second copy of the Act toward me. Crowley grabbed his wrist.

"Everybody must sign," said the Major.

"A child of his age is not competent under law to give a binding signature. Check with your legal department. If you want to engage his loyalty, let him loose in the torture chamber at the Tower of London for a whole afternoon. He would boost the morale of your Yeoman Warders."

Underworld

A chauffeur drove us all the way to London and dropped us down a joyless alley, not far from Downing Street. We entered by a huge building through a door that was hidden by sandbags and two soliders took us into a lift.

"It is unusually slow, isn't it?" said my father.

"It's very deep," said one of the young soliders.

I got more and more restless as the descent went on forever.

"Is Dame Nelly Melba going to sing," asked Crowley, "or shall we be shovelling for coal?"

We stepped out into a busy road junction, a second Piccadilly sunk into the bowels of the earth, with tunnels leading to all points of the compass. A shrunken railway track ran in front of us, coming out of one tunnel marked 'Central' and going down another marked 'Outward'. There were scores of signposts but three I remember because of the odd mental images they provoked: Clapham Deep, Kent Artesian, and Chalk Farm.

There was a distant rumble like the noise of machinery or of buildings falling. It came from far away and overhead. "If I'm not mistaken, that sounds like bombs," said my father. "Just the tube trains," said the taller of the two men in khaki. "The District Line passes within yards of a higher level. It makes a very good escape route if there should ever be an emergency."

"While you're at it," hissed the Major, "why don't you tell them about the special cemetery."

"Sir?"

"Where we bury fools who choke on their own tongues."

The soldier's lips clamped into a thin white line and his jaw muscles set like cement. I must have turned a shade paler myself because the Major squeezed my shoulder. "Only joking," he murmured. But I wasn't any too sure.

17
UPUHAUT

A wolf-headed god who opens the way to seekers

The Admiral
There were about ten people in the small conference room. One of them, who wore the uniform of an admiral, pointed to the cheap wood chairs and the trestle table. "Please sit down. In spite of all and any evidence to the contrary, the furniture does serve its purpose — but only just."

"Perhaps now, we will at last learn the reason for our being here," Crowley nudged.

"Yes, yes of course. Sorry to have been cagey. Matter of fact, our back-room boys have come up with a quite diabolic scheme. Hitler, as you doubtless are aware, is a confirmed consumer of the sort of thing that we British reserve for fun-fairs or the Golden Mile at Blackpool."

"Do you speak of sea-side rock?"

The Admiral inclined his head and one could almost hear him murmur touché. "I speak of the beyond, Mr. Crowley. It seems the Der Fuhrer never acts, never takes decision, never does anything important, unless he first obtains the counsel of his pet astrologer. Mr de Wohl here has a duty to ensure that we benefit from identical advice. Luckily for us, of course, he has some personal knowledge of the very man that Hitler trusts. It seems they were on amicable terms before the war."

Crowley seemed rapt in admiration of his own finger nails. "I regret to say that I am quite unable to amplify on Mr. de Wohl's astrological insights. If you thought that I spent my nights looking at stars, your intelligence gatherers have made a mistake."

"Far from it, Mr. Crowley — our files and dossiers are sound, solid and secure. Packed with quite useful tit-bits, most of them — chock full of highly interesting facts. For instance," he drew a manilla folder toward him, "we know everything about you and the groups you have belonged to. For example: The Celtic Church, The Spanish Royalists and we must not forget The Hermetic Order of the Golden Dawn. Ah!" He pointed at the page with his finger. "Someone has found it worth noting that in the Zelator grade, an aspirant must learn the Nazi salute."

Aleister waved his hand airily. "Merely a druidic gesture to hail the god of the sun."

"Quite. Quite. But who might he be, Mr Crowley, keeping it in mind that the Nazi swastika is itself an image of the sun, inverted? Indeed, some scholars trace the world to Sanskrit, su asti, which means: good being. Then there are others who hold that it means star of the east, that is to say: the sun." He let that sink in for a moment. "All the same," he went on, "it is curious that so many occult orders have German ramifications, don't you think?"

"You must not confuse any of those with Ordo Novi Templi, the Order of the New Templars. That is an extreme racist movement which began in Austria."

"Where Adolf Hitler was in fact born." He smiled quietly and picked up a standard War Office pen. "No doubt it can be explained away as a string of odd coincidences." He smiled again and twisted the pen round and round like a propeller. "You and I though: we know different, don't we?"

Assault on Asgard
"You are that strange, unsettling type of man who is both an idealist and an opportunist. Not all that unlike our dear Herr Hitler, I would have thought. No offence, dear chap. One sees at once that you have quite a different code of morality. Do you call it morality when you're an occultist, I wonder?" He slid the pen gently between the clenched fingers of my father's hand. "At all events, I can promise you this: if you endorse our project, all the old rumours would stop. And it would be proof, if any were needed, that you are not and never have been a Nazi sympathizer."

"What about the Freemasons?" asked Aleister. "Can you keep them off my back?"

The Admiral shook his head regretfully. "God could, no doubt. But up to now, He has chosen not to."

"Which God are we talking about?" asked Crowley.

"Beaverbrook or Northcliffe?"

Crowley wrote his name at the foot of the sheet of paper. "I have signed away my soul for all I know, could you now tell me what the hell it's all about?"

"One could indeed. Our boffins want you to have a cover name, some other way of referring to you without betraying your true identity. It makes very good sense. Walls have ears, as they say. We have a special list and I can easily allocate you one from that. Unless of course, you have some name you wish to propose?"

Crowley thought a moment and then said: "Old Mother Clutterbuck."

The admiral's eyebrows shot up and he lifted his head slowly. "May one ask why?"

"It was a comic character in the only pantomime I ever saw as a child. It is a very fond memory. And think how funny it would be to hear civil servants trying to pronounce it with their usual gravity."

"Quite!" The man coughed. "My name is Triton, by the way. Mr Louis de Wohl is known as Cassandra. As for our chief," he waved an invisible cigar, "he is known as Johann Sebastian or JSB for short." He paused a moment to wait for the obvious query. There wasn't one. "Bach," he said weakly.

"His bark is worse than his bite."

"We shall call the boy Aladdin," said my father.

Had he been standing, I am quite sure the admiral would have reeled. "Does he have any part to play in this?"

"Perhaps yes, perhaps no, but we may well need to borrow his magic lamp!"

Triton suspected his leg was being pulled, but couldn't be quite sure, so he wrote down the names exactly as Crowley spelled them. "You come highly recommended by a certain Mr Maxwell Knight[1], an important figure in the country's secret services. Mr Churchill sought his advice, you understand. Consequently he has asked for you by name."

"JSB," said the other. "You see what a good memory I have."

"He will expect a report each day. They say that he reads everything in bed at night. At all events, he will send back crisp,

---

1. Masters A. *The Man who was M: Maxwell Knight*, Basil Blackwell, 1984.

pithy, not to say caustic replies. When everything is ready, he will come and say a few words."

"A sort of toccata and fugue," mused my father. Then he tilted his head to one side and regarded the admiral rather oddly. "If JSB is taking a personal interest," he said slowly, "then it must be very, very important?"

"Quite right," agreed the other, "which is why we decided to call it 'Operation Mistletoe'. The allusion being..."

"It will surprise you to learn," said my father, "that Old Mother Clutterbuck is quite well versed in Teutonic mythology." He studied the other coldly and very calmly. "Am I to take it then that our target is Balder?"

Darling of the Gods
Balder was a handsome young god in Valhalla, the son of Odin and Frigg, and greatly loved by all the other gods. His mother made every creature promise never to harm him. But she omitted to ask the mistletoe simply because it looked too frail to be of any danger. But Loki, the evil god, persuaded a blind man to throw some mistletoe at Balder during a game. That is how Balder died.

There was one of those long silences that seem to last forever. "We have already spoken of the swastika and the druid salute." He was still twirling a pencil between his fingers, as if he were scared of what he had to say. "There are many other Aryan symbols, the runic sigil of the Waffen SS for example. Taking all of these things together, the idea emerges — or the interpretation could be made — of a planned attempt to involve or invoke the powers of darkness[2]." He sniffed and rubbed the tip of his nose.

"The cold brutality is not just a rumour of war. The sexual excesses of all kinds are more than a vague story. Even the murder of babies! I'm no expert, God knows, but a lot of all this obscenity appears to have close rapport with a certain category of occult ritual. Add to this the fact that women are tacitly inferior to men, here only to provide pleasure, babies and food. And add the concept of men as superior beings whose ancient destiny is first to be heroes and finally to be mutated into gods." He looked at us with gaunt eyes. "And what have we got?" he asked. "What

---

2. Goodrich-Clarke, N. *The Occult Roots of Nazism,* Aquarian Press, 1985.

does it mean?"

"Armageddon," came the hollow croak from my father, and far away another underground train rumbled like thunder in the offing.

They did not move for a while. Neither of them much felt like speaking a word. Their faces were bleak. There was just the sound of them breathing. The admiral was the first to break the mood.

"Well, Old Mother Clutterbuck," he even attempted a grin.

"We haven't got much to joke about. So let's try to delve into the heart of the matter."

"The top members of the Nazi High Command share a great deal in common, but they differ quite remarkably as individuals. Many of them, maybe even the majority, are deeply involved in magic and occultism. Several of them who have been party stalwarts right from the beginning, but a number of these were members of secret societies a great deal longer still. Now, a number of these organizations were linked to, or shared similar origins with, the Order of the Golden Dawn. Hence the name of Aleister Crowley is quite renowned in their circle[3], one might even say honoured, in some cases. Now each member of the High Command has been studied. Each has his own taste and penchant when it comes to occult doctrine and the practice of magic. Balder, you guessed right — that is how we refer to him — Balder will favour secret doctrines that are very like your own. Hence you will understand how best to influence him, and he will be that much more impressed when he knows that you are involved. This is the task which faces us, my dear, Old Mother Clutterbuck. Of all the top brass who surround Hitler, which one is most receptive to you?"

Two Germans

It took about four hours to reach R.A.F. Tangmere travelling by official car from London. We were due to meet two German officers; code-named 'Kestrel' and 'Sea-Eagle'. The whole thing had been set up between the Roumanian Mission in London and its counterpart in Lisbon and was all very hush-hush. I'd been quite excited at first, thinking of a spy film I had seen. But I grew tired

---

3. Brennen, J. H. *Occult Reich*, London 1972.

and bored before we even reached the outskirts of the city. Crowley offered to teach me chess but very soon snapped the box, and his mouth, shut! Funnily enough, it was almost the first thing that either of the two Germans said. "You play chess, I hear?"

I was not looking at him. I was treating him with all the contempt that the enemy deserved. The German was very polite but his accent sounded silly. I decided to keep an eye on them and if they tried to escape, I would help the Home Guard recapture them.

The remark had been addressed to my father, and he nodded his head carefully. "In that case, Mr. Crowley, you know that the King is not himself the most powerful piece. One loses, one wins or one reaches a stalemate. And then one turns to the next game." He cleared his throat nervously. "There are players, Mr Crowley, and there are those who plan their strategy several moves ahead. There are dabblers..." He raised his shoulders.

"And there are Masters," said my father, finishing the sentence for him. He made a special sign with his hands. The two Germans bowed their heads in salute or in reverence. "We regret the need to conceal our identity," apologized the other German, "but our lives would be in danger."

"But we know who you are, Herr Professor, Herr Doktor." This from Triton, who didn't care to be left out of the conversation. Those two words, professor and doktor, stuck in my mind but only because I had read comics which featured mad professors, and I had seen a German Doktor in the film about Frankenstein. When I delved more deeply, many years later, I learned that the professor was Karl Haushoffer, a significant figure in German occult circles, and the doktor was Joseph Retinger, who held high office in German Freemasonry and who later joined the Polish Free Forces in London.

But the Germans appeared slightly miffed by the Admiral's slip of the tongue. "Of course you know who we are," he agreed, "or this meeting would not have been allowed. But it was clearly understood there would be no photographs, no names, and no use of titles, my Lord!"

Crowley gave a huge grin. The Admiral gave a polite nod and sipped his tea. There was more in this than meets the eye, as I will explain a little later. The German picked up the thread once more. "Our Country is not very old, you understand, and our history is not so rich in tradition as your own. Even so, many are very troubled by what is happening, some are quite alarmed, and a few, the older families, are ashamed." He looked straight into our faces and his eyes were bright with sincerity. "This is not easy to say. The last war was asinine but at least there was honour. Afterward, it was our own fault, our own sense of being publicly humbled, that we allowed a lunatic to lead us." His voice cracked and he turned his face into the shadow. The first German took up where his friend had left off.

"We have come to be traitors and that is hard. We would like you to know, my comrade and I, that we are not cowards." "One does understand," said the Admiral calmly, "but all private feelings aside, do you understand what it is that we expect of you?"

Both men nodded. The other one turned back into the light. "To go on with the chess analogy, you want us to sacrifice a piece. We speak on behalf of many others who would like White to win. We agree." He fished inside his hat-band and gave us a piece of paper. "Here is your Balder's name." Crowley looked, the Admiral looked, they looked at each other with eyes on fire.

"Well!" said my father.

"As you say," said the other. "Time, I believe, for the fairy to wave her magic wand!"

It was the only time I ever saw Crowley use his fist to give a right upper-cut.

18
MENTHU

The bull-headed God of War

Supper at Arundel
Our next visit was to the cathedral at Arundel where we met a man whose name, I assumed at the time, was Mr Mighlawd. He was in fact a bishop and Dean of the Vatican's Diplomatic Corps. He did not seem at all uneasy to be in the same room as Crowley, and they looked at each other with rather more interest than one might have expected. Both sides, I could tell, were wondering how to get things started, when the bishop himself asked a rather silly question.

"I am told, Mr. Crowley, that you have something to do with English Freemasonry?" He spoke with a foreign accent and it was impossible to say whether his remark was deliberately offensive or merely the result of some careless briefing. Crowley, who had no great love for the Catholic church, was in no mood to give the bishop any benefit of doubt.

"No, My Lord. You are probably thinking of my associate here." He indicated the Admiral. "But I have it on very good authority that your Lordship's church has some connexion with the German soap industry?" There was a stunned silence in the room. Crowley was referring to two things: the Vatican's failure to condemn Hitler's treatment of Jews and the rumour (if rumour it was) that human fat from concentration camps was being used to make soap. As I've already remarked, my father was a dab-hand at choosing the exact spot to shove his knife in. He showed no qualms whatsoever for the outrageous statement, but smiled and nodded to people round about as innocently as a lamb. From this moment on, neither of the two men spoke to each other directly. They addressed their remarks exclusively to Triton, the Admiral. He did the best he could to handle the situation, like Mr. Speaker in the House of Commons — keeping the two sides from each other's throat.

We were there for the simple reason that the Catholic Church had a vested interest in the outcome of the secret operation. Someone higher up, probably Johann Sebastian Bach, had had a few words with the Apostolic Nuncio. This was not motivated by any sort of diplomatic courtesy. The important thing was that the church had an understanding with Germany. It also had personnel who had access to, even contact with, people who were in the Nazi High Command. It would be very, very helpful if we could persuade the church to... no, not help us, but... afford us certain facilities.

But there was a fly in the ointment. While the church had not been given all the crucial details, it did understand that ritual magic would be involved in one way or another. That, the Nuncio explained, made the church very unhappy. In no way could it allow itself to be seen as condoning or turning a blind eye on the use of devilry. This was why we are all meeting at Arundel, at the cathedral attached to the Duke of Norfolk's home. The Duke of Norfolk is the hereditary Earl Marshal of England and always acknowledged as the leading lay Catholic of the country.

The bishop began to probe for reasons and explanations. These were all supplied because the case had been very well prepared. It was emphasized with great vigour that the British Government did not believe in magic, as such. But certain high-ranking members of the Nazi Party did, and that was the crucial point. As far as we were concerned, any acts we might perform would be empty and meaningless. ("Speak for yourself!" I heard my father mutter.) But ways would be found to ensure that chosen "target figures" would get to know all about it.

The bishop mulled all this over for a while and appeared to be satisfied. "There remains one last question," he confided. "We wonder what might be the political attitude of your Mr. Crowley? Does he, for example, favour the left or the right? In which direction do his personal views incline?"

The Admiral's eyebrows shot up as he looked anxiously at my father. "The bugger has bowled a googly!" he hissed. "I haven't the slightest idea what to tell him!"

Provocations

Aleister himself stepped forward and, without looking at anyone in particular, made a solemn pronouncement. "If the very reverend prelate is asking about my private colour preference, pray assure him that I detest *red*! You may also add that I feel very much more at home facing God than sitting either at His right hand or His left."

A flicker of a smile lit the Bishop's eyes and he raised his hands, clasped as in prayer, toward his chin in order to hide his lips. "May we be assured," he asked a moment or so later, "that there will never be any public recognition of this operation?"

"None at all," said Triton.

Crowley found this reply a shade too quick and a great deal too humble for his own liking. He threw out his chest and drew himself up in a way that made him massive and awesome. "But that is not to say," he drawled, "that I may not choose to mention it myself."

The whole of the Catholic delegation went stiff with alarm. Their heads went together as they conferred confidentially in Latin.

"Mr. Crowley is merely joking, Your Lordship." The Admiral's steely glance warned against any contradiction. "He is quite celebrated for his outrageous sense of humour." The Admiral turned to face my father and spoke with enormous gravity. "He knows full well that if he did anything so foolish, first of all we would simply ignore him. And then, after a due interval, he would vanish into the bowels of the Tower of London. No judge. No court. No appeal. Just a short journey in a covered van."

Crowley regarded him coldly. "Ah," he commented. "So you do have royal connections?"

He had told me long before this, that we knew someone who was related to the King. At the time, I didn't realize whom he meant, but I was quick to pick up this little jibe. Even so, he may still have been joking.

The Admiral frowned at Crowley severely. "Could you just for once in your life stop acting the damn goat! This country is at war and the government has unlimited power to act as it thinks fit. Your flamboyant egocentric tom-foolery could cost us millions of lives."

"So sorry," said Crowley, in the forced voice of a repentant child. "I couldn't resist putting the wind up him. It did my old heart good."

A Bishop Translated
The bishop overheard this exchange and drew his own conclusions. He got up. No, one couldn't just say that he stood — he rose to his feet as if were robed in his full, carmine canonicals. He advanced toward Crowley for all the world as if he were descending some marble sanctuary steps designed by Raphael or Bellini. Although he wore a simple black suit with a stock and collar, we could all but hear the rustle of silk. He nodded to the Major but then, he extended his hand to Crowley. On one finger there shone a splendid ring. Crowley took the hand in one of his and, instead of raising it to his lips, he studied the rign like a jeweller. Then he produced his other hand from behind his back. On his finger there gleamed an even bigger and more impressive ring. He gazed straight into the bishop's eyes. "Swap?" he suggested roguishly.

The Bishop laughed and even clapped his hands together in applause. "So then it is true, Mr. Crowley: you are a joker!" "In many games, My Lord, a very important card. But being so otherworldly, you may not have realised." With that, rather impudently, Aleister bestowed an occult blessing.

The bishop's face was wreathed in a huge smile as he clapped his hands on my father's shoulders. "Oh, Mr. Crowley," he mused with a slight sigh. "I think you would be surprised at how much I do realise." To everyone's shock he bestowed a different occult blessing on the speechless magician and embraced him.

This may bewilder readers today as much as it bewildered us then. The Bishop's name was Angelo Roncalli and help is provided by a book from a reliable Catholic source. In *The Broken Cross*, Piers Compton states that Roncalli became a member of the Illuminati sect while he was on diplomatic service in Turkey. He later became the Patriarch of Venice, being given the red hat while on a visit to France by President Auriol. In 1958 he was elected Pope John XXIII. On his pectoral cross he even bore the sign of the Illuminati — an all-seeing eye in the centre of a triangle.

Piers Compton, I should add, is the former editor of the Roman Catholic newspaper, 'The Universe'.

Ashdown Forest

It was Pythagorus, I think, who said he could tilt the earth if given a long enough lever and a fulcrum. What Aleister Crowley did as regards the subsequent history of the world was every bit as momentous.

The high ritual took place at a spot in Ashdown Forest, Sussex. I must not say where exactly. Despite all the security, word did get out but in a twisted version, and ever since, the locals have been pestered by weird people. Crackpots come, even some Nazis, apparently to suck up any magical energy that might still linger. It was Gerald Gardner (about whom, more later) who shifted the story to the New Forest. That would have been further away from the target we were aiming at, and along the wrong Nexus, vis-a-vis Germany. The ceremony itself was long and complex. I have lost a great many of the details mainly because certain items were so dazzling and prominent. For instance, I have a very vivid memory of a dummy, dressed in Nazi uniform, being sat on a throne-like chair. I had to sit with my back to this, and a large mirror was raised in front of me. The result was I could see my own face quite close, and the dummy's face over my right shoulder.

Most of the people there wore occult robes of one sort of another. At Crowley's orders, even the contingent of soldiers had them over their customary battle-dress. I say robes, but in most cases they were mere lengths of sheeting. Each of them had a runic symbol cut out of coloured felt and stitched on to the breast. "With the right connections," my father would say, "you can often get felt, even in wartime!" The mass of people moved around the dummy and me in two circles. The outer one turned deosyl and the inner went widdershins i.e. with the sun and against the sun. This movement wasn't just a regular, monotonous rotation either. At certain moments, or at given signals, they wove in and out of each other. It reminded me of the furry-dance I had seen in Cornwall, or the figure dances in the film of 'Gone With the Wind'. It was all timed with great precision, and each time the dancers stopped, and faced inward, the runes on their robes spelled a different set of messages which were all aimed at the dummy.

Aleister explained that the gist was quite close to the short phrases I had to yell out, each time the dancing stopped. They were not in English nor in German but they signified things like: You are the one appointed, and You are the hero armed in gold. There was a lot more like this, but all of it in a similar vein. Strange names and weird titles cropped up from time to time and I recall how irritated my father got when I had difficult with the word "Thule".

The Bird Flies
At the climax of the ceremony, bird-like wings were clamped on to the dummy. It was hoisted to the top of a church tower and, after being set alight, it was launched along a cable in the exact direction of some special location in Germany. It ran only a few hundred yards of course, and it dropped bits of burning rubbish along the way. A squad of R.A.F. firemen were detailed to follow its track and to quench any outbursts that it caused. It didn't get as far as the tree where we had anchored the cable. "Not long enough and a bit too much droop," explained Aleister wickedly. It dropped onto a narrow footpath and caused a small blaze. It was quickly dealt with and only three or four small trees were blackened. The flight path, if that's not being too ambitious, had been planned so that it went nowhere near any remote cottages or isolated buildings.

Everyone was sworn to secrecy beforehand and again afterwards. They did their best, I suppose, but rumours did get out and strange memories have not only lingered, they have grown. Word has it that the forest is a favourite haunt of black magicians and witches' covens, and that something "very nasty" happened there forty or fifty years ago. Some of this may be the result of misinformation that was deliberately planted. At all events, the tale has got terribly tangled in the telling. Amateurs of secrets, and perhaps a few practitioners of occultism, do still tramp around the region, armed with pendulums and trained psychics.

One or two occult groups with fascist leanings are also on the hunt. They are trying to scavenge any residual energies that might still be lying around. If it's power they want, they'd be much better off raising their own instead of trying to swab up that split by others nearly half a century ago. Ours was all but used up. Any remaining traces would be so minuscule you'd need forensic tests to identify them. This is certainly the true explanation for mysterious happenings so well described by others.[1]

It was some time later, the 11th may, 1941, to be exact, that my father received a telephone call.

"Is that Clutterbuck," asked the voice.

"Old Mother Clutterbuck, to be precise," said Aleister.

"Triton here. The sea is calm. The bird has flown! Balder is back from Hel."

When the news first broke in the newspaper headlines, the whole nation was stunned. "Hitler's Deputy Quits the Reich", trumpeted one. "Rudolf Hess Flees to Britain," blared another. But my father was among the first to be given the news. He closed his eyes and bowed his head as if he was moved, or as if he were saying a prayer of thanks.

---

1. Collins A. *The Black Alchemist*, ABC Books 1989.

19
MAAT

The goddess of truth and justice, the abstract principle deified

A Nation's Gratitude
"It was agreed, you remember, that there can be no medal nor any other kind of award. Johann Sebastian is sure you will understand. He asked me very particularly to express his and the nation's thanks." There was a few seconds silence. "Apart from the agreed fees — is there anything else we can do for you?"

"What about making me Court Magician? Couldn't you pull a few strings?"

We heard the admiral's smiling sigh. "So sorry, old boy. Afraid you'd be recognized going in and out."

"Isn't there a back-door? The place seems big enough."

"Got to go, I'm afraid. Over and out."

"Over and out?" shouted Crowley. "Can't you find any cheerier way of saying goodbye? Listen to Old Mother Clutterbuck, dear boy. At very least say 'Up and Under'?" The telephone clicked and went dead. "And him a sailor," mused my father flatly. "I'd always heard they were oversexed. Or is that just the ones who sleep in hammocks?" We had a party of fish and chips, all washed down with scrumpy. Aleister was over the moon. So much so, he danced a jig and gave himself a slight attack of asthma. "So," he wheezed with pride. "We damn well pulled it off! How about that, eh? It worked, it worked! By all the prunes in Scotland's sewers, it really and truly worked!" He flopped into a large arm-chair.

"Well, well, well! Imagine that! Mind you, it's not the most important thing I've ever done. But by the beard of Hatshepsut, it's a rare moment of triumph these days." I looked up Hatshepsut in my favourite encyclopedia by Arthur Mee. It turned out she was Queen of Egypt about 1500 B.C. The Egyptian monarch, whether male or female, wore a false, ceremonial beard on state occasions. I could only think that Aleister was poking a bit of gentle fun at himself. He had long since renounced his youthful obsession with things that hailed from Egypt. "The esoteric path," he instructed, "should not need to be exotic as well!"

Silent Witnesses

Rudolf Hess spent the rest of the war in prison. Later, at the Nuremberg trials, he told one of the doctors (D. M. Kelley) why he had fled to Britain. He had received spirit messages, he explained. Toward the end of 1940, these had become more and more urgent. The gods were demanding that he did something because he was the Chosen One, the new messiah. He alone could bring a new age of peace to the world. He was Balder, whereas Hitler was the evil demon, Loki.

It was on this evidence that the allied medical team began to doubt Hess's sanity. Consequently, he was not sentenced to death along with most of the Nazi High Command. He was condemned to life imprisonment in Spandau.

After Hess's flight, Hitler purged magicians and seers throughout Germany. He started to run the war without the magical assistance that he had valued so much up to now. He dare not even rely on his own psychic powers. So whereas he once used to know things in advance and make decisions with astonishing success, he now made blunders, the displaced energies affected his brain, and his conduct of the war began to go badly wrong. In fact it was the beginning of the end.

The strange thing is that no one has ever been able, or permitted, to offer an explanation for Hess's defection. No historian, no scholar, no expert on war has ever come up with a viable theory. Even so, most of them agree that it is one of the greatest, unsolved mysteries of the Second World War.

No doubt my memory is coloured by the elation we all felt the night of the Great Ritual. More significantly, I was only a child and, let's admit it, a child's memories can get mixed up or even magnified. So if I make allowances for all that, then the hundreds of people I seem to recall were probably more like sixty or seventy. The 'Marx Brothers' were there — the small, the tall and the fat — as was Gerald Gardner. So too was Maxwell Knight, a top figure from the British secret service, who many thought was the model for 'M' in Ian Fleming's "James Bond" books[1] He was directly involved in the operation but much more than that — he had a profound, personal interest in occultism and was terribly excited to watch the ritual unfold. Years later, when all the spy scandals were breaking, I often wondered if there wasn't some connexion. After all, despite their militant atheism, the Russians were actively pursuing research into psychokinesis and a force which they labelled "bioplasm".

Odic Forces

Why has none of this ever come out? It's quite a puzzle, isn't it? Not once in fifty years has anyone said a word. Yet other matters have been revealed and some of them, once closely guarded secrets, have been made into films like 'The Dam Busters' and 'The Man who Never Was'. They were hush-hush too, but they came out in time, when there was no longer the slightest reason for keeping them under wraps. Evidently, there are people who felt it is absolutely crucial to go on keeping the Crowley/Hess story under wraps, even today. As far as they are concerned, it is still a very hot potato!

Rudolf Hess is dead now. Nobody is quite sure how he died, least of all his own family. There was something of a mystery about it all. It was presented as a suicide but it was not that straightforward. Hess's own son was indignant and outraged, but because Spandau was controlled by an allied commission, he could not obtain any legal access. According to the son, his father showed no signs of depression and never spoke of suicide. Indeed, he still protested his innocence and occupied his time in writing. One can understand this. A man does not wait in prison for fifty years before deciding to end it all in extreme old age. He is more likely to compose his memoirs, don't you think?

The newspapers sifted through the ashes of old stories but found little new to say. One or two kites were flown, hints were dropped that the K.G.B. has known something about it all along. But without something new to add, you can't keep the old fire burning. The mystery gave a final splutter and then died down.

1. Masters A, *The Man who was M: Maxwell Knight,* Basil Blackwell 1984.

The cameras moved on and the story was buried in the archives. Which is exactly what they wanted. Russia and the United States were members of the commission that ran Spandau. Both had a military presence. And throughout the post-war years, both had conducted scientific research into the strategic potential of certain occult or psychic force which they called Bioplasm or The X factor[2]. Since 1845 though, when it was discovered by Carl von Reichenbach, the Germans have always called it the Odic Force. After the god Odin, you see... who was the father of Balder.

Double-cross
In my opinion, there is nothing in my account which can possibly salvage Aleister Crowley's reputation. This Operation Mistletoe doesn't actually show him in any better light, for he seems to have been a bit of a reluctant hero and somewhat mercenary as well. But then again, who wasn't? It is not difficult for those in power to create whatever impression they wish. They have the means and they have the motive. Was the hallowed figure of Winston Churchill all bulldog, pure patriotism, and nothing else at all? Eisenhower, Montgomery, De Gaulle — unmitigated heroes whose golden images will shine forever? It wasn't so with the First World War. The images of Haig, Foch and all the rest — flaking, rusty, and becoming more transparent.

It would be nice to imagine they have kept the wraps on Operation Mistletoe simply to deprive Crowley of merit. They wouldn't want him as any sort of hero, of course not. But the reasons behind the silence are far more complex and grave. There was a lot more going on than many people realized. Crowley knew. He got his information from the two "good" Germans that he met at Tangmere. It was this secret briefing which persuaded him to play it all for real and not just go through the motions.

Let me raise the curtain once more. The last act was played a long time ago. The actors' contracts have run out. A new audience applauds new productions in a world where fame counts a great deal more than talent. But as regards Operation Mistletoe, there is still the denouement.

---

2. Ostander S, Schroeder L: *Psychic Discoveries Behind the Iron Curtain,* Sphere Books 1973.
Walker, B. *Beyond the Body,* Routledge & Kegan Paul, 1974.

in fact, I would be surprised if they will be that obvious. That's what will happen in Pall Mall, of course, in all those gentlemen's clubs. They will sip another port as they ride their armchairs toward oblivion. "Humph," they will cough. "It never happened." But don't the dear old fools remember? Rudolf Hess did flee to Britain and no explanation fits as well as mine. In fact, no other explanation has ever been put forward. Humph! to you, too.

But where are all the silent witnesses? Why have none of them ever come forward? Many of them are dead, of course — and most of them were not unknown to the gentlemen of Pall Mall. Dennis Wheatley, a former member of the Secret Service, a former associate of Aleister Crowley, who helped him with his famous black-magic novels. Wheatley did a complete volte-face and started attacking evil right, left and centre. In one of his later books, 'The Devil and All His Works', he reviles Crowley thoroughly, whilst at the same time goes into every detail possible. The book was not motivated by philanthropy however; it's price in 1971 was £2.75! Ian Fleming was there too — yes, the man who later wrote the James Bond books. Not to mention Tom Driberg, the Labour M.P. and Rear-Admiral John Godfrey. But some of you are still alive. Ex-civil servants, former soldiers, even friends of Aleister Crowley. You'll be in your late sixties, at the very least, and I don't believe for a second that any of you have forgotten.

Oh please don't pretend that its the dreaded Act again. Others have broken it. People in positions of confidence in Whitehall and former members of Military Intelligence have published and have become rich. But not on this one subject, never on Operation Mistletoe. How long will you pretend that nothing happened? How long can you go on pretending to be good little boys who do what the bigger boys tell you? They got very scared that night of the ritual, didn't they? And if they got scared, my God! you were terrified.

Something happened that you hadn't counted on, that you never even suspected. There was a certain group, wasn't there? And it's members were not just interested in depriving Hitler of his source of secret power. They were aiming to steal it and use it for themselves.

Crimson to Purple

I cannot drop things there. The enigma might frustrate the reader and make him so cross that he will view the whole kit and caboodle as hogwash. On the other hand, I am deeply involved. I have to be careful how far I go. At present I am merely a thorn in their side. I also possess things they would like to get their hands on. But if I go beyond a certain point while discussing things in public, their anger would be so great, they would try to stop me at all costs. Even if it meant abandoning their search for Crowley's secrets.

I have pondered things very carefully and I have decided I will present you with a list of the key-facts. It is up to you to establish the necessary links. What I am about to say is serious. This is not a stunt, like that jewelled rabbit everyone went digging for some ten years ago. What I am about to say has nothing whatever to do with weaving fictitious, romantic plots. These are facts:

— the Head of MI5 was deeply interested in occultism
— on his recommendation, Churchill asked for Crowley
— Bishop Roncalli was a member of the Illuminati
— Arundel is the home of the Hereditary Earl Marshal of England, one of the great Officers of State
— a member of the royal family was supreme head of English Freemasonry
— before Crowley was involved, it had been decided that the operation would be magical and Germanic
— during 50 years of imprisonment, Hess gave no useful information, according to the official line
— Hess died in strange circumstances while engaged in a lot of writing
— after the war, there were a great number of spy scandals in all the allied countries and West Germany
— one of the main accusations in the Philby affair was to do with the betrayal of our spies in the Eastern bloc
— Hitler believed his destiny was to re-unite the pure and perfect race of people
— Hitler was advised and surrounded by occultists
— Freemasons were behind the French Revolution when the monarchy was destroyed
— Napoleon came from nowhere, stopped the chaos, and built a European empire. He was a visionary and used occultism
— Both Hitler and Napoleon led charmed lives until they

turned their backs on the source of their power
— the Masonic symbol on the American dollar bill was ordered by President Roosevelt in 1945
— Churchill and Roosevelt held a meeting behind Stalin's back at which they planned to re-instate the old Hapsburg Empire as a bulwark against the tide of communism that would follow the end of the war
— The man proposed as Emperor was Lord Louis Mountbatten, the admiral. He was a direct descendant of Queen Victoria and closely linked with the Romanov dynasty of Russia itself[3]
— In 1960, Queen Elizabeth II changed the name of the Royal Family. It had been the House of Windsor.
It is now the House of Mountbatten-Windsor.

That is not everything, but it is enough. If some of these statements seem irrelevant, or appear to float about like loose ends: why not try plaiting them?

---

3. Michael Howard, ib

20
BASTET

The cat-headed goddess of music and dance, who protects her people from contagious disease

Witch Queens

Witchcraft does the very best it can to deny any viable link with Crowley.

"He was not a witch," one lady[1] says. "He was nervous of wicca with its feminine bias, him being gay since his best friends were men."

Her argument stretches over three whole pages which, like the church condemning the Templars, is overdoing it a bit. Not that she ever met him in person, you realise. She gains her insight by a steady sifting through all of his works that are still in print. This lady has a talent for breaking codes that no one knew were there. With her gift for innuendo, she could earn a very good living writing scripts for television. All that's missing is "Nudge, nudge. Wink, wink. Know what I mean?".

But the Aleister Crowley she describes: is this the same man who is supposed to have called up demons? Is this the same magician who became infamous for seducing women at the drop of a hat, or anything else that was loose? Is she referring to that rake, that braggart, that shameless upstart who was never known in all his life to be in any way reticent about his sex life? This man, we must remind her, was the begetter of some five or six bastards, as well as a quantity of legitimate children. Or is she perhaps implying that we all came by air-mail or special delivery of some sort? In either case, we don't need crystal balls to tell she doesn't much like him!

1. Valiente, D. *An ABC or Witchcraft Past and Present*, Robert Hale & Co. 1973.

Fair play, boy-oh! If that is the kind of game we're in, witches too leave themselves wide open to similar slurs and sarcasm. They have chosen the ground-rules without perhaps realizing what gorgeous figures of fun they make. But there is no need for sly allusion in their case though. We can simply state the facts and leave people to draw their own conclusions. For example, what kind of religion is it that insists on total nakedness... while at the same time requiring that a garter be worn?

Just to go one step further, why do they describe their state of nudity as 'sky-clad' and claim that this is humankind's natural state? I must say that this seems astonishingly naive of them. I do agree, yes, that babies are not born fully-dressed. But this is simply because the mother's womb is not a front-loading washing machine! What with all the coils and other gadgets being used for contraception, that day may yet come, but the well-known, and often badly tailored, birthday-suit is just a matter of economy.

What a giant step forward for mankind it would be if we were born fully kitted out. But you see: we don't actually care for nudity except for that re-discovered pagan festival called 'the summer holiday'. Even then you risk being toasted if you go too far south, and there's a danger of frostbite if you go too far north. At either extremity, we might lose the bits which are necessary for survival. Even in the fairly moderate temperate zones, you have fog, smog, hail-stones and acid-rain.

Add to all of this the fact that the standard-issue birthday suit does have a tendency either to wear out and/or to sag like an old mattress and — no, I'm sorry — but nudity is not on. A newly hatched chicken starts prouting feathers. A newly born rabbit starts to grow fur. A newly arrived baby means a rush to Boots, Mothercare and the local knitwear shop.

Night-hags

Then we have the amazing broomstick over which the witch cocks her leg.

During the poverty of the 19th century, and up until just after the Second World War, an indigent couple could jump over a broom to enter into a sham marriage and so avoid the expense of a real one. In the North and many other industrial areas, they used to call it "living over the brush", and neighbours would oblige by turning a blind eye. Otherwise, the broomstick is a universal symbol for hags who have traffic with spirits and who go riding out to meet them. But "riding out to meet the spirits", like "ride a cock-horse to Banbury Cross", does carry some obvious sexual allusions too. When we get down to brass tacks, it really means entering into a state of trance by means of erotic stimulus — not all that far from "getting high, man" or "I'm having a trip".

The author herself admits most of this, but insists that the true significance of the broom is a symbol of ritual cleansing. Well, one of the best books on the subject[2] says this could be true... but only in Japan, apparently. As for that cheeky garter, Miss Valiente's book has no special entry on the topic. Why is this? Witchcraft stipulates that this is the only 'garment' that can be worn — yet in this important book no explanation is given. Maybe that is because we are now on shakier ground.

Garters, as witches probably know, were exceedingly rare in the days before stockings had been invented! This doesn't stop them trotting out the totally unproven theory, first proposed by Margaret Murray, that the English Order of the Garter, founded by Edward III, was a flimsy cover for a witch cult. When there is a simpler explanation for the facts, we are wise to prefer it.

In those far-off days, garters were not elastic. Elastic had not been invented. We hadn't heard of rubber. Garters were very long laces or leather thongs, which were wrapped criss-cross round the leg and then tied. Now if one of these dropped to the floor while the poor, dear Countess of Salisbury was dancing — it was a pretty safe guess that she'd already been unfastening them during the last few minutes. In other words, Milady had been playing hanky-panky! It is now much clearer why the King said "Honi soit qui mal y pense": he was the one who had not retied the knots properly. Not that anyone would have been terribly shocked, in any case; they would have admired both his gallantry and his choice. Evidently he was no liar — just a fumbler. Like George Washington, he told the truth but — he was clumsy with it.

Witches say that they wear the garter as a sign of rank. There's nowhere else that they wear pips or sew on chevrons, I suppose, and the garter is just about the only thing that does not wobble

2. Cooper J. C. *Illustrated Encyclopaedia of Traditional Symbols,* London 1978.

or swing about on a blustery night. But whatever reason they care to give, it has no real basis in antiquity.

Magic Ointment
Last but not least, we have each witch rubbing down her colleagues with a kind of greasy ointment. Once again, the alleged purpose in this kind of neighbourliness is a mystic flying of the mind or an uplifting of the soul. Well, there are certain drugs which can be absorbed by the skin. In veterinary practice you pour them in a tiny trickle along a cow's backbone to keep her free of worms, ticks and liver fluke. I'm not aware of such need among witches.

There is also the famous 'oil of camphor' which is used by elderly folk to rub on to rheumatic muscles and arthritic joints to help relieve the pain. The one my mother favours is called "Firey Jack". Well, even though they dance in the nude under the stars, I've not heard that witches creak more than the average person.

At the other end of the age-scale, we have all those applications used by teenagers to tackle adolescent skin problems such as acne and other unspecified spots. Plus, of course, the lotions put on babies' bottoms to help keep nappy-rash away. To be thorough — and Miss Valiente was very thorough — we also touch on that special religious oil used by Japanese Sumo wrestlers to foil an opponent's grip. But I am not suggesting that witches are either incontinent or given to close-quarter combat.

Finally there is the sacred chrysm that is used to hallow Kings during the coronation ceremony, and also to sanctify the bodies of the dead and dying in the office of 'extreme unction'. No disrespect but I can see no connection with witches.

Perhaps I have been approaching things too literally? To understand properly, maybe we must read between the lines? It is quite obvious to any fair and decent minded person that witch activities could never be compared to the goings-on in Soho, Montmartre, or an Italian beach at midnight. I'm not narrow-minded. I'm a man of the world. I don't want to misjudge people. So, being as generous and candid as possible, I believe we all get up to a bit of witchcraft now and then. We just don't call it that.

As for men being Crowley's best friends: we could say the same of Napoleon, the Mafia or the Grenadier Guards! It is a matter of scientific fact that the majority of dudes spend more time comparing notes with each other, than they do in yelling Bingo! Women are lovely for sleeping with, but men make better friends. Did you know, by the way, that Lesbians are much more common? The fascinating thing is that their numbers have grown along with the advance of feminism. Of course, no statistical link has yet been demonstrated, if you'll pardon the pun.

Valiente is not alone in casting doubts on Crowley's virility. Several male authors have proposed a similar idea. But in 1967, the law of England was changed and homosexual acts are no longer criminal. No one has thought fit to tell the police yet, so when they are not fighting terrorists or defending high street banks, our boys in blue risk their all as decoys in men's urinals. But despite all this, spilling the beans no longer horrifies the public. A man is no longer ruined.

But the lady's hatchet job on my father falls to pieces. In one sentence she casts doubts on Crowley's sexual tendencies, and in another she mentions that he and Gerald Gardner were *very good friends*. This is really interesting because dear old Gerald Gardner is reputed to be the father or inventor of modern witchcraft. As a matter of fact he was not, but that's neither here nor there. But what a stunning revelation! The Most Wicked Man Who Ever Lived on intimate terms with Our Beloved Founder? Did they have pet-names for each other... 'Gerry' and 'Al' for example?

Quite unwittingly, the lady has provided a clue. I think we should follow it up.

Antique Origins

The word witch, derives from an Indo-European root, weik. This becomes wicca or wicce in Old English, witche in Middle English, and witch in the language we speak today. This word has to do with magic and sorcery. But there is another Old English term, wican, which has become weaken and weak today. It is this root that is being used in witch-elm and witch hazel, for example. According to the scholars, there is no possible way that the modern term 'witch' can be derived from any Old English word meaning wise, or wise one. Wizard, on the other hand, does mean either a sorcerer or something dried-up and wizened. So much for philology.

Witches[3] claim that they are either the relic or the revival of a

---

3. Sweet, H. *The Student's Dictionary of Anglo-Saxon*, 1896, Oxford.

fertility cult that is some five thousand years old. One feels that a cake is called for and one chorus of 'Happy Birthday to You'. To support their claim, they cite from the work of Charles Leyland[4] and Margaret Murray[5], neither of which produced the slightest drib of evidence to back up their ideas, and both of whom had their ideas rejected outright by the majority of established scholars[6]. These two authors relied far too much on surmise and wishful thinking. They allowed themselves to be misled by their personal enthusiasm. That is putting things in the kindest light possible.

But their books sold very well and they have been tremendously influential. One could say exactly the same for 'Mein Kampf' by Adolf Hitler, of course, which just goes to show that there is no clear relation between popularity and truth! Had it been otherwise then we'd all be directing our prayers toward the factory that makes a certain laxative. What *is* true is this: average folk make the most crucial decisions in life by asking: "do I like it?" It is the same phenomenon that lets anglers catch fish. The brainless creature looks at the dangling maggot. He doesn't ask how on earth it got here or why its got a hook through its guts. No, "do I like it?" and swish, he's in the basket! That is how the weirdest of cults grab their converts.

"You have only to start," said Crowley, "and witchcraft will spread quicker than nits!" He was having a head-to-head chat with the same Gerald Gardner that I mentioned earlier. In the long course of history, gods have sometime failed and men's hopes have been thwarted. When this has happened, the dilatory gods were sacked and new ones set up in their place. Truth was not the issue but "what good has it done for me?" A bit like politics, in fact. Anything that lasts must be ipso facto better than most, which is why new brands of occultism try to acquire a patina of dust and antiquity. Your average idiot thinks it survived only because it worked well. The ad-men know it. "This beer helped to put out the Great Fire of London!"

Our life is short and we are conscious of mortality. This is why we have certain reverence for history and the origin of things.

4. Leyland, Charles A. Aradia, or the Gospel of the Witches, New York 1899.
5. Murray, M. A. *The Witch-cult in Western Europe,* Oxford 1921.
6. Rose, Elliot. *A Razor for a Goat, Toronto 1962.*

Sacred shrines were almost always placed near burial grounds. Altars were often grave stones. The paraphernalia of ritual was often seeds mixed with bones, or semen and blood. The past is known, but the future is not. The courage to face tomorrow comes from the glory of yester-year — the new buds spring from old roots.

This is the reason why modern witches in Milton Keynes leap across the centuries and claim direct descent from Morgan le Fey or Merlin!

Why does it Exist?

We all have ancestry or we wouldn't be here. Only the aristocracy keeps a record of names because they need to prove 'ownership' from time to time. Don't let it worry you though. Take heart. Allowing for only four children per brood, and just four broods per century, a pocket calculator can demonstrate that the world population is descended from the French King Dagobert! This provides a new insight into books like 'Holy Blood, Holy Grail'[7]. But heirship via the eldest male child is a matter of politics and not religion. It is of interest only when you are carving up power and land; it has nothing to do with the way we distribute truth. We are all heirs to divinity and every man and woman is a star if only because human beings are descended from that very first amoeba which swam in the primaeval slime. In some cases, it shows.

At any rate, it is a quite common practice for writers on occultism to make a claim to antiquity to make their concepts seem valid. You know the sort of thing: *and so it has been, since the dawn of time, one generation after another*. There is a case to be made for worshipping the human knee-cap. It too is millions of years old and it carries the mysterious name 'Patella'. If age alone was the thing that mattered, then certain sandwiches would be the object of pilgrimage at several London stations.

But it doesn't matter how much I mock them. In the realm of mysticism, there is no truth like an old truth. Despite the dominant feminine influence, witches commit one of the oldest mistakes in the kitchen, alas. If a pinch of pepper is good, they say, then

---

7. Baignet M, Leigh R, and Lincoln H. Jonathan Cape 1982.

a wagon-load must be better. Just lift the lid off the cauldron: you'll see straight away what I mean. A bit like school-dinners in wartime, there is too much spice and nowhere near enough meat!

If you try to study witchcraft, the first thing you'll notice is the total lack of material to study. Oh yes, there are lots and lots of manuals about what you can do, but nowhere is there a book which explains the doctrine or the reason for doing it. There is praxis but no theory. We are looking at a religion which does not possess a theology. Oh I don't doubt that someone will leap for his pen or word processor the moment he reads my words — but this is a bit like inventing the motor-car after you've been trying to prove that inner-tubes were current at the time of King Arthur and his Knights of the Round Table.

The essential question is: what is the point of witchcraft? Why do witches do the things they do? I haven't the slightest doubt that they get a lot out of it but... is that enough? Does that suffice as a raison d'etre?

21
MIN

A god of fertility and harvest, a protector of travellers. One of his marks is an erect phallus

Gerald Gardner
It seems that women were very much taken by Gardner. It also seems that he very much enjoyed taking them. Not to make too fine a point of it: he had something of a name for it. One bright, sunny morning, he announced that he had gained a doctor's degree during the night! Only his partner could tell us how he achieved this, but perhaps she was at a loss for words.

I joke, of course. A bit of tit for tat, if you'll pardon the expression. Crowley is good game for witches, and when they poke fun at him their aim is to discredit him as a serious magician. All I'm doing is just tipping the balance in the other direction for once. If we put all grudges and bitterness aside and try to be perfectly honest, then a person's private, sexual tastes having nothing much to do with magic.

To some folk, if not to most folk, decency means pretending that the nastier things in life do not really exist. Decent people hide things. They put lids on toilets, locks on doors, and stick to dictionaries which are free from all four-letter words. It's their own business. It has nothing to do with me unless they try to turn their views into law and restrict my own personal liberty. I happen to believe that they will pay a high price for their anti-natural hypocrisy. They will cause themselves biological stress and suffer psychological conflicts.

Among other things, being a pagan means that you let off steam. You release the pressure and unblock the flow of energy inside you. This means you are free to focus your attention on the creative aspects of your own nature. In this respect, nudity can be an effective way of getting rid of shyness, of gaining self-assurance, and of shedding all the hang-ups that are to do with sex. After we've said all that though, there remains the matter of truth... spiritual truth. As I talk about Aleister Crowley's role in all this, I fear a few feathers will get ruffled.

Valiente says that Gardner admired Crowley's poetry so much that he used bits of it his witchcraft rituals. She also says that the rituals Gardner received had gaps in them and that this poetry helped to weld them into a coherent system. She goes on to assert that Crowley's offering did not really amount to very much at all. But, if you remember, earlier on she said that he had never made any at all! It seems we are making progress. But how odd, to put it mildly, that none of this was mentioned in her section about Crowley. This new insight is slid in sideways under the heading about Gardner. But at this point she makes a little mistake. She says that Gerald Gardner met Crowley in 1946-7 during the last year of Aleister's life. That may well be true. I have no grounds for denying it. But what she omits to mention is that they first met several years earlier! I can tell you that they had known each for quite a long time. As a matter of fact I saw them together in 1940! I was actually introduced to Gardner and invited to call him Uncle Gerald.

The Commission
"I am toying quite seriously with the idea of reviving the witch cult,", said Gardner.

Crowly gazed at him calmly for several seconds. "You might just as well make love to a dummy in Harrod's windows." He sniffed airily. "How can you possibly revive that which has never existed?"

Gardner ignored him. "Margaret Murray believes that it was rife in pre-history."

"Margaret Murray is somewhat rife herself!" snapped my father. "It would do her reputation more good if someone would take pity and give her a kick up the arse. Like many of the academic ladies I have known, she makes up for her prim personality with a fertile imagination."

"Your own imagination is not exactly sterile," said the other.

"Touché!" said Crowley with a slight smile.

"In fact," Gardner went on, "that, together with your vast knowledge of magic, might be just what I'm looking for. Yes, yes, it might very well do the trick."

My father's attitude changed at once, from that of a tolerant barman to that of a stockbroker short on clients.

"Tell me, dear chap," he murmured unctuously. "How costly a trick have you got in mind?"

Gardner did some quick totting up. "Oh, shall we say... one guinea per page?"

"Shall we say three," said Aleister, "With double spacing." And that is how it began. That is how the witchcraft movement was launched. The two men, glasses in hand, discussed it as coldly and calmly as the producers of a West End musical. Once the finances had been agreed on, they got down to the finer detail. Crowley was sixty-five years old at this time, and he had a gift for this sort of thing.

"We must have nudity," said Gardner going red.

"But not too much," reminded my father. "Don't overdo it or you'll defeat your own ends! Even caviar would cloy the appetite if it were served first course, second course and every bloody intercourse!" He roared and banged Gardner on the back. "You know what I mean," insisted the other. "A touch of the erotic!"

"Nothing is more erotic than doffing and donning, putting on and taking off. Have you never noticed how much tastier the turkey looks before you start slicing it? That's what raises the power, dear chap: anticipation!"

Both eager and afraid, Gardner wallowed in a froth of conflict. "Yes," he said. "I see you are right. We must not go too far."

"Don't you worry," Aleister assured him. "The heavy accent on the feminine side will veil things very nicely. On the other hand, things may get slightly Dutch."

"Dutch?" asked the other, puzzled.

"Full of dykes," chortled Crowley. "Mannish ladies in tweeds, brogues, and Eton crops! It wouldn't upset me in the slightest, but how would you feel?"

"I want to liberate women," said Gardner. "I want to give them their proper role in magic." He saw the twinkle in Crowley's eye. "Oh come on, man. You know what I mean." "I hope you know what you're doing," replied the other.

"Remember Baron Frankenstein: built his monster, but misplaced the spanner that would tighten his nuts!" He laughed again, quite liking the joke he had made. "After the war, I doubt if women will go back to being second-class citizens. That's where you come in with your witchcraft — no doubt hoping they will honour their debt of gratitude."

"There is more to it than that," hissed Gardner, going red.

"My dear chap, would I dare impugn your motives when they so closely resemble my own?"

"Don't let him kiss you," hissed Crowley as I escorted them to the door. "If he has had malaria, you will be taking quinine tablets for the rest of your life."

Crowley Gate

They concentrated so much on "goings on", the two of them quite overlooked the need for some doctrine to justify it all. Crowley was content to put magic within reach of the ordinary people. Gardener published 'Witchcraft Today' in 1954 by which time Crowley had been safely dead for seven years. I wrote to protest about some of the claims he made. Of course, he never replied.

An author[1] who likes witches says that their induction rites must stem from those of ancient tribes. But someone more impartial[2] writes "any scholars state that Crowley, rather than Gardner, is the true father of modern witchcraft". The '161 Laws of the Craft' are supposed to come from a 'Book of Shadows' dating from the sixteenth century. It has been proved, he says, that the first version was written by a friend of Gardner! Before it appeared in 1958-9, Gardner just redid the language to make it more archaic. That friend was my father. I can vouch for this because on more than one occasion I was allowed to join in. "He is in puberty," said Aleister, "bursting with lyrics of lechery, and how charming it would be, the touch of a naive innocent, eh?" Uncle Gerald made copious notes and these he worked up into a grimoire soon afterwards. This is now kept in the Ripley's Collection at Toronto.

Gardner was frisky, amusing and not short of money, so my father buttered him up with both hands. He enrolled him as a member of the Golden Dawn, shifting the date back, and granted him a charter for forming his own chapter of the O.T.O. Like leaders of banana republics, either man could always find room for

1. Donovan, F. *Never on a Broom-stick,* Allen & Unwin, London 1972.
2. Rusell, J. G. *A History of Witchcraft,* Thames & Hudson, London 1980.

another medal or one more exalted title. Legend has it that Gardner was made a witch by "Old Dorothy Clutterbuck", who mounted rituals in the New Forest to thwart a German invasion. I have already explained how the ritual happened somewhere else, for a different reason, and that "Old Mother Clutterbuck" was a pantomime dame whose name my father adopted.

Well, there you have it. That is how it really came into being. A Great Beast, an old Goat, and one scallywag aged twelve. None of which should destroy the faith. It had to start somehow and no matter what the original motives were, truth is able to manifest itself when needs be. Nowadays, there are pagan groups to satisfy all tastes, and many of them are pursuing goals that are far away from spiritual. For my own part, I respect and esteem those who have approached the hidden door I mention below.

Research was done[3] to find how people reacted to a prophecy that turned out to be false. They joined a sect whose leader had revealed the end of the world. But when it did not arrive, the people felt fine. Far from feeling let down, they thought that their prayers had been answered. I have shown their founder in a truer light, but witches will believe what they want. They will adjust to what I say and none of it will destroy their faith. They will feel that I am hostile, I suppose, and may try to attack me. It is what one does when one is angry and hurt. But when passions have cooled and reason has returned, the truth will be waiting to be faced. Perhaps it is hard to swallow, but my story fits all the known facts. Above all, I have no wish to cause harm or distress. I am trying to set the record straight. So money changed hands, what does that matter? Gardner was not the true author, what difference does that make? Crowley did his best, he was a magician; who is to say he did not succeed?

The Secret Door
Wicca was meant to be alluring and be a lode-stone for people who were timid, lonely and frustrated. It was meant to provide a pretext for men and women who were too scared to make whoopee. There was nothing at all wrong in that. As far as it goes, that's fine. But there were also the "Right Ones": sincere souls who

---

3. Festinger, L. et al, *When Prophecy Fails,* University of Minnesota Press 1956.

would come searching for guidance and light. As I said earlier, Crowley made quite sure that there was a built-in secret door. Why? Firstly, he had a childish streak and it is precisely the sort of thing he would do. Second, he felt obliged to offer a true goal and not just a sensual game. In short, what he did was serious, but how he did it was playful. The "Right Ones" would explore a bit more deeply and look further, he hoped. If the going got difficult, they could always be helped. The door could not be stumbled upon by accident because, unless one was deserving, it simply ceased to be.

Let me make this point quite clear. The craft as it stands is not an adequate key. But a way of passing beyond will show itself to those who prove their worth. Witchcraft is something more than a pleasant pass-time for folk who are too scared to look beyond their nose.[4] I see it as one among several other starting points which lead in to The Mystical Search. One Saturday in August, 1972, my students moved through Trafalgar Square, sorting out seekers who had come to find me. I was there myself, but in a better disguise than Dustin Hoffman in the film 'Tootsie'. A nice witch came straight up to me and warned me that journalists and men with cameras were hiding behind King Charles' statue at the top of Whitehall. I hope her life has been good. People like her are to be admired for their sincerity and their gentleness. I have great compassion for those who have been misled but, as with other routes, there are cheats and deceivers. Faith does not actually need proof — so be very chary of anyone who offers it unasked.

---

4. Argyle, M. *Religious Behaviour*, Routledge & Kegan Paul, London 1965.

22
RENPET

The goddess of springtime, youth, the seasons, and the year's passage

Are you Ready?
"It will be your birthday before very long," he told me one day. "You will be twice seven years. That is an important crossroads." He had already mentioned things of this sort before but as the date drew nearer, he became more agitated. "I think it is appropriate that you become an Initiate." I can't say that he seemed over the moon at the prospect. I wondered if I'd failed in some way. I looked at his glum expression. "I'm sorry if you're not quite sure that I'm up to it." I suggested bravely. "I've tried my best to stick to all the studies but I have school work to do as well."

He mussed my hair and gave my shoulders a hug. "It's not that," he reassured me with a smile. "It's something else. The day you become an Initiate, our ways will separate. You will have to go on with your own life, alone. You will have to prove to the Gods that you are as apt as I have told them." He held me in his arms again and I think there were tears in his eyes. "I have vouched for you, young man. Once you are an Initiate, we shall never meet again in this life."

He wouldn't explain things any further than that. I had to trust him. He was always right. So when he held me at arm's length and studied my face, I knew I was being etched in his memory. "You wouldn't understand how glad and proud I shall be to perform the rite. But because I am your father, I must be seen to do my duty well and without bias. In other words, I must be sure that you are ready. If I initiate you too soon, it would be worse than putting a curse on you."

"My grandma thinks I'm ready," I told him boldly. Somehow or other I thought that this might help him. As far as I know, the two of them never met, neither did they have any contact. But she figured a lot in his earlier schemes. She'd contributed the gipsy blood, after all. What's more, he'd been quite content to leave my upbringing in her hands. I felt she mattered to him in some way. That is why I told him what I did.

"How do you know this?" he asked quietly. "How do you know that your grandma thinks you are ready?"

"She said I had gone beyond."

He drew his breath in slightly, but his facial muscles betrayed nothing. "And what was it that made her say a strange thing like that?"

I thought it was going to sound silly. I hadn't told anybody else but her. "No matter where I go..." I mumbled, "I hear the sound of footsteps following me."

He paused. "A child molester," he mused. "An agent from MI12," he offered. "Or quite possibly both?" I smiled at his little quip. "Didn't you realize that the British police force is a haven for undesirables? If you're the right height and don't need spectacles, anyone can get in. Believe you me, son: The CID are only one step from being criminals themselves, and there isn't the slightest doubt that the Secret Service pullulates in perverts and pederasts." History has since proved him right, but then he was at Cambridge! He drew out his pocket chess board and idly laid it flat. "We can't place too much weight on footsteps," he murmured, studying the board.

"But I have looked. I have used shop windows and I have laid traps. No one is ever in sight."

"But you'd expect them to be good at disguises, wouldn't you?" He moved a pawn from one hole to another. "The army can make buildings invisible and hide huge tanks by camouflage. Highly skillful I grant, but not uncanny!" He yawned slightly. "Anything else?"

"I know things before they happen."

"What sort of things? You forecast night in twelve hours while eating your breakfast? You suggest it will rain after the thunder has rolled?"

"I knew about the war, didn't I? I knew it was going to start!"

"So did everyone else apart from Mr. Chamberlain!" This was the Prime Minister who tried to pacify Hitler and who believed until the very last minute that we could still have 'peace in our time'.

I was beginning to feel cross with his sceptiscism. "When my father hanged my dog, I told him he would get hurt at Dunkirk."

"So you say, but that was a long time ago. Nothing more recent?"

I was silent a moment. I wasn't quite sure if I dare say it. But one way or another, I had to convince him. "I know when you will die," I announced.

The Mark
Aleister's hand was poised over the chess board and he didn't falter for an instant. "Do you know when *you* will die?" he asked as he lifted the black Queen.

"No," I said honestly. "But I believe that you do."

"How interesting. And what, pray, is the date for my own demise?"

"You know that too. That is why you made me when you did, at the chateau near Boulogne. That's the reason you led me toward the hidden doorway."

He closed his eyes at precisely that moment, and he seemed to shiver with pleasure, like someone making love. He breathed in very deeply. For a moment I thought his asthma was starting. "What have you seen?" he asked in a soft, tremulous voice. "Did anything strange happen to you in the last few weeks?"

I didn't want to tell him. I wasn't bothered about becoming an Initiate. I just wanted to be friends and not have to go away. What made it worse to bear: he never said why this had to be. In my private anguish, I tried to think of all the possible reasons. But I didn't get very far. It was futile to ask. I'd tried that. "It is hard enough making decisions, without having to explain them!" That was the only answer I got.

With my school-boy imagination, I started fearing the worst. Was he shielding me from a curse? Was his soul about to be claimed by the devil? Was it simply his age, and he wanted to hide in the frailty of his declining years? If the truth be told, he wanted me away and hidden before his enemies found out about me.

To be fair to his memory, I never witnessed his alleged addiction to drugs. He told me quite openly that there was only one way to relieve his attacks of asthma and that was by smoking a herbal cigarette containing stramonium.[1] The stench was so dreadful it could have shortened the war by years. I don't think these were of very much help to him. When he started up his bag-pipes — which is how he described an attack — he just quietly left the room and came back a minute later sounding very much better.

He didn't disguise his pleasure in alcohol either, but I never saw him drunk. Yes, he relaxed, got slightly merry and became very humorous, but he never lost his self-control. I was not there all the time. I only knew him during seven years. So I'm in no position to dispute what others may say. They may know better... or perhaps they have better reasons for speaking ill of him. Or it could be just a myth. If so, it is worth wondering who started it and why.

"Becoming an Initiate is a great step forward," he said, "which must be taken at the proper time. The arrogant try too soon. On the other hand, the gutless try too late and sprawl arse over heels at the threshold. Judge well if you wish to be well judged yourself. Not too proud, not too fearful: climb when the moment is ripe."

He bowed his head and tapped the top of the closed chess set. "Now let's see. Where were we? Ah yes." He regarded me curiously. "I asked if anything had happened during the last few weeks."

So that is when I told him about the sand-pit.

The Sand Pit
We were too poor to have a big house. It was a one up, one down in a back street, facing a mill. Since there was no quiet corner where I could do my homework, I had the habit of setting off on my bicycle, if the weather was fine, and looking for some spot in the country. I knew every wood, field, high moor and by-road even better than the A.A. man. There was one gloriously bleak spot, that looked just like the film of 'Wuthering Heights'. There I could not only do my maths and Latin, I could even practice my *magical voice*! Oh yes, Aleister had loaded me with work too and I had a mental list of sites that were suitable for both academic

---

1. This is the dried leaves of datura, the same drug said to lead to mystic visions by Carols Castenada (cf. *The Teachings of Don Juan,* University of Calif. Berkeley, 1968).

and arcane activities. In this way I did my magical drill, did better and better in my school subjects, and also watched a couple making love! What you might call a good, all-round education!

One afternoon in late spring, I was riding along in a bit of a daydream. The classroom had been hot, the lessons had been boring, and my head was feeling heavy. All in all, I wasn't in a very good mood for either history or the manufacture of iron. I'd been along this lane before so it wasn't all that strange, but this time I was surprised to stumble on a side-track that I'd never noticed. The opening was all but hidden by the overgrown hedges which had been left uncut for so long that they almost met in the middle! How curious that I had missed it at other times! How strange I should find it now. Well homework or no, I could not resist exploring. Off I went.

I edged my front wheel off the main road, and pedalled slowly through the weeds. It was not much more than a cart-track: twin ruts where the wheels had gouged for years, and a raised central ridge of docks, thistles and hemlock where only the horses walked. I followed it on a meandering course for something like half a mile until it turned right abruptly, and ended in an old, disused sand-pit which had also served as a rubbish-dump for a few scattered villages.

Here and there were fascinating piles of waste and the contents of domestic dustbins. Mounds of broken furniture, car bodies and farm implements. Plus a terrible stench and one or two darting grey rats that dived into tunnels. There was the deep buzzing noise of clouds of fat flies, and the cawing of crows which were cross at my arrival.

It was strange, out of the ordinary. I didn't feel any menace at all. There were no signs or notices, and nothing was marked dangerous. It would have made no difference if there had been. To me, this place looked a bit like an Aladdin's cave and I was anxious to start rummaging for treasure.

I'd been standing astride my bicycle. Now I cocked my leg off and began bending down to lower it to the ground by the handlebars. That's when it happened. I felt paralysed. I felt as if the column of air over my head had become extremely heavy. I felt an enormous, growing force pressing down. I thought I might be ill — a bit faint perhaps — needed a drink. But still I couldn't move. Every muscle and every bone was locked.

The next thing I noticed was that all noises ceased and all movement stopped. It was as sudden as if a lid had been slapped on a stewpot. No flies, no breeze rustling the trees — just nothing. Neither did anything move. The clouds stood still in the sky. Branches stopped swaying. I felt like part of a painting. I was merely a photograph of a boy caught in the act of lowering his bike to the ground. I don't think I was frightened, not yet. I was too amazed. I could hear my own heart pumping and I could see my chest rising and falling as I breathed. And there was just one, faint gurgling sound from somewhere inside my belly.

The Hand
Then all at once, I knew I was in a presence. That's not an expression a boy would use, I know. Yet that's how it felt. There was something there beside me, something huge, something mighty, and my skin started tingling just like the time we did electrical discharge experiments in the physics laboratory. I could even hear tiny crackling noises and I could see over my forehead that my hair was standing out like a ball. I moved my eyes downward and gawped at my shoelaces which were rearing up as rigid as sticks!

Now I began to sweat. I wasn't hot. I don't think I was tense. Nevertheless, I could see my skin expressing droplets of water as if I were being squeezed like a ripe orange. It trickled down arms, legs and body. I was soon wet through. Then the air round about me started to thicken. It's the only word I've ever found that gets near enough to the sensation. Imagine you were swimming in a bowl of milk and it started turning to cream — well that's what it was like. The invisible air became invisible jelly. It was as if some strange being was slowly taking form. Then, as my eyes grew wider and wider, all the plants round about me started to bend. The brambles, the bracken, the grass and the dandelions — they went flat, absolutely flat — as if they were being pressed down. And I could see a shape in their flatness. Nothing solid, you understand, just the impression on all that vegetation of a huge, open hand.

I stared at the imprint of the gigantic fingers. It dawned on me very gradually that I was standing right in the middle of the unseeable palm.

I don't know how long it lasted. I can't even guess how long

I was standing there, frozen and stupified. A few minutes? An hour? Just a split second? There was no way I could judge or estimate. Subjectively, it seemed to last a very long time indeed, and throughout it all my mind was flooded by enigmatic images that zipped by like the view from an express train.

Then, when it had become almost bearable, the great weight faded. The outline of the hand lifted and the blades of grass and stems of plants rose upright again, unbroken, just as if nothing had happened. Reality came back, not as swiftly as it had gone, but one bit after another as if some technician were switching on the different circuits in a certain order. The noises returned, the movements, and I... unfroze.

It was like waking up, and more like falling back to sleep again because this world, my world, was nothing compared with all the things I had appreciated in that other world. My surroundings were just as they had always been before, but now they seemed drab and uninteresting. I backed off slowly, guiding my bike. Once I was some ten yards off, I stood on one pedal and waltzed away. Now the fear struck me! The further I pedalled, the stronger the fear became. I went quicker, and quicker, careering through the outskirts of the town, and practically falling into our little house. My mother and grandma jumped up in alarm. I must have looked a sight! They listened wordlessly as I babbled out my story. I was still panting for breath, and when I'd finished the two women looked at one another, my Mam questioningly, my Grandma knowingly.

"He's thirteen!" said the old lady as if that explained it all.

The next day, she gave me her beautiful pack of tarot cards, more than a hundred of them, all hand-painted and quite unique.

"Here," she said. "It's your turn to have these. Hand them on when the time comes."

23
TA-DHENET

The peak, the mountain: a name for the snake-goddess of Thebes otherwise known as Merseger

What an Initiate is

My father's chess set lay on the floor where he had dropped it. As he heard my tale, his eyes had blazed and he had become more and more excited. He asked me to repeat a tiny detail. He asked about the distance to the nearest village, and was there running water in the vicinity. He brow-beat me as if I were the chief suspect in some terrible crime. When had I last eaten? Where was the sun in relation to my face? Had there once been any kind of mining in the area? And so on, and so on. I began to wish I'd never mentioned the subject. But as we went on, Aleister became a much happier man.

"Well, that's it!" he said finally. "I'm pleased to tell you that you now bear the mark. My boy: you are ready to become an Initiate."

I looked in the mirror at a small mole I have on my left cheek. "Is that the mark you mean?" I asked.

"Nothing so obvious," he laughed. "It's a token which announces that you are not as other men. It is a sign that says: I have put this one apart." He looked at me steadily and took both my hands in his. "You have been chosen by the world beyond."

"Chosen for what?" I gulped, remembering what I'd read about human sacrifice and such.

He explained that being a magician is a job just like any other. You learn the ins and outs. You collect the tools and practice with them. And you pray to the Gods to find you the right teacher. "Fortunately," he added matter-of-factly, "I am the best teacher in the world!" Which I dare say he probably was. The teacher's job is to uncover your latent talents and develop them. He's not there to amuse you or be kind to you. His sole purpose is to get you as far forward as he can in a given time.

One begins then as a learner, more or less with 'L' plates on, and you are not let loose to practice magic until you have reached a certain level of proficiency. Granted, I was extraordinarily young to qualify as an Initiate, but don't forget I had been studying for seven years and with a first-class teacher. (It took twenty-years altogether before I was summoned to be a Master).

The point of becoming an Initiate is that one is then a qualified craftsman — one can do, one can help, one can try to advance the Great Work. Instead of just studying, you can perform services for others. That is very important and highly rewarding. The people who make it their living to write about occultism seem to assume that the Great Work is some kind of re-construction of a mythical Golden Age. Well, while many groups do use the symbol in precisely this way, true occultists view things slightly different. We want to remove the unnatural forces in the world and allow nature to resume the process of evolution where she left off. In some societies, the Freemasons, for example, they might speak of "the restoration of the Temple". But we, the true occultists, have no intention whatsoever to banish indoor plumbing or to forbid false-teeth. There is something rotten in society, but we don't necessarily destroy society to root it out. In other words, we are not disguised anarchists.

"Becoming an Initiate," said Aleister, "is a bit like being made a prefect at school!"

I think he was being sarcastic.

Apprentices

All joking aside, it is an important step in one's magical career to rise from Student to become an Adept. It is far more than a mere change in title or status. From this point on, one can look to the Gods for direct, personal help. The other world commonly bestows new gifts and powers, all of which the Initiate must learn how to control and use. In olden days, when trades were mostly to do with manual skills, it was co-ordination of hand and eye, or the knack — one never changed one's job. One was admitted to a guild and one stayed "a brother" for life. In modern times there are many intellectual professions which, once learned, leave your hands and time free to feel dissatisfaction and boredom.

Yesterday, magicians had a role in the community: they ministered to others. Today, those others are likely to want to study magic for themselves — in order to make up for something lacking in their lives. Very few of these people wish or need to become Initiates.

After spending such a large chunk of his life as a student, the end of an apprenticeship was marked by an elaborate send-off. It helped the new craftsman fix the change in his head. It helped the community to acknowledge the step upward he had taken. In short, there were 'rites of passage'. In the case of coopers, the young man was tarred, put in a barrel of feathers, and rolled about the workshop. A brewer or tapster might be drenched in ale and have a special 'tap' stuck on his penis. There was often an overtone of sexual mockery — as if obtaining a trade was the last touch toward begin recognized as a man. The boy stops being a boy and joins the warriors. In an African tribe he might well be circumcised without anaesthetic. Whereas in the guild of carpenters he might be nailed by his trousers to the rafters. Among some coal miners, he was carted off in a filthy state to his girl-friend's address and she was required to give him a bath.

"In one particular trade, I understand the lad is auctioned off to the highest bidder!" laughed Aleister.

"Am I allowed to choose?" I asked archly.

He looked at me with amusement. "The idea behind a lot of this horse-play is that — one way or another — you must prove that you are a man."

Despite poor wartime food, I was quite tall for my age. The sap rose late for most boys and they tripped badly when they heard the first cuckoo of spring. I, on the other hand, had been where the bee sucks and lain among the cowslips for several months already. "You don't have to worry on that score," I assured him. "There is some toothpaste in my tube."

He laughed so long he almost triggered his asthma.

Reckoned by the formula thirteen plus seven in the seven, the day was fixed for 29th September, or Michaelmas. By an older calendar, it is known as the autumn equinox. He piled on the amount of last-minute study, and I had to plough through several books in the few days that remained: The Egyptian 'Book of the Dead'; 'The Life of Buddha'; The Tibetan book, 'Bardo Thodol'; 'The Analects of Confucius'; and lastly, the 'Kebra Nagast' of

Abyssinia! Not one detective story among them.

I had to follow a regime of strict personal hygiene too, watch what I ate, be careful how I dressed, guard my tongue in company and, very importantly, regulate my hours of sleep. Each of these things was just irritating in itself; taken en bloc, they got on my nerves. In the end my self-control cracked, and I told him bitterly that it was all stupid.

"Don't be a baby", he rebuked. "You're getting off lightly because of your age. It's nothing compared to what you'll have to face later on in your life!"

The Stone Circle

It was one hell of a job finding the right place to hold the ritual. With typical grandeur, Aleister had even considered Stonehenge, and only threw the idea out because it was too close to the army. What with tents, tanks and Tommies, the whole of Salisbury Plain was awash with khaki.

A well-meaning friend suggested the Tower of London simply because legend said that the head of the God Bran was buried there. "Why not Tyburn Tree?" asked my father with withering scorn. "It is in the middle of the road near Marble Arch. The precise spot is marked by a commemorative plaque!"

"That's a great idea!" replied the other, not catching on.

"You don't think that perhaps we might just cause a traffic jam?"

St. Alban's cathedral was also proposed, not because it was a shrine to the first English martyr, but because Alban had also been a pagan druid. However, the place was too close to the town centre and would attract a lot of unwelcome interest.

"One fool even suggested Lyons Corner House!" groaned my father. "It is often hired by Jewish families to celebrate a Bar Mitzvah!"

"Does that mean you've not found anywhere? Is the whole thing off?" I asked, a shade too eagerly.

"Not at all," he said. "It is on!" He patted my empty stomach patiently. "Not much longer to go now. You'll soon be as fit as a fiddle, and when it's all over, I'll treat you to a slap-up meal."

"Any chance of a small sample in advance?" I was truly quite dejected. I don't think he realized that for a growing boy, fasting felt more like starvation. I knew it was all important to him so I manage to rustle up a slight display of interest. "So where is it to be? Where will the ritual take place?"

"We shall stay with friends in a remote corner of Oxfordshire, not many miles from the village of Little Compton."

"Never heard of it".

"That's as may be," he said. "But it is quite well-known in occult circles."

"What's so special about it?"

"There is a ring of standing stones which the locals call The King's Men.[1] The legend says that marauding Danes were heading south to steal the crown of England. A sorcerer stopped them by turning them into stone." He saw he had caught my interest and smiled. "Strange things happen there. No one sees anything. They turn a blind eye. Many of them are still loyal to the old ways, you see. They don't look when they're not supposed to look. They close their doors and they close their minds."

It was not as big or as impressive as Stonehenge, but these stones were supposed to be much older. Individually they were quite small, scarcely the height of a man, and they hadn't been worked at all. They were just plain stones planted in the ground. Yet they were splendid and they did throb with power. One of those mystic gateways is situated quite close to the spot.

When I visited the stones, I 'saw' a man being killed. Two years later, the 13th February 1945, Charles Walton was murdered in Lower Quinton. His neck had been stapled to the ground by a pitchfork, his throat had been slashed, and a billhook had been sunk into his ribs.[2] Seventy years previously, a similar murder had happened in Long Compton. Local folk said they had both been wicked men who had put spells on people by sending out frogs attached to miniature ploughs, with harness made from human hair. Neither case has been solved. No murderer has appeared in court.

They knew more than they say in those parts. During my military service, I was stationed quite close and they recognized me. I often went there 'for a real dinner', and we talked about things. I learned that the murders had nothing to do with revenge. Both of them were a settling of feuds between rival sorcerers.

1. cf. Bord J. & Bord C. *Mysterious Britain*, Garnstone Press 1972.
2. Detective Superintendent Robert Fabian of Scotland Yard later wrote a book about this. See also McCormick, D. *Murder by Witchcraft*.

As if to confirm matters, I got a postcard via the internal post at my camp. On one side there was a picture of the Rollright Stones. On the other side were the words: "You must forget"!

The Strange Boat

The costume I wore was a kind of kilt or wrap-over skirt that came down to mid-calf. The fabric was a lustrous gauze, flimsy at the hem but heavier higher up. There was a loose shift of the same material, and a pair of gilt sandals.

They helped me into a small reed-boat. It was like a canoe except the ends curled up and were decorated with beautiful red tassels. Once seated, four costumed men raised the litter to their shoulders and carried me down to the cellars. A man in the mask of a long-beaked bird was waiting for us.

When the other had gone, he showed me a balance. There was a chair on one pan and a painted sarcophagus on the other. When I was seated, he opened a nozzle that allowed sand to trickle from a cistern into the sarcophagus.

"Your time of testing has begun, and will last while the sands of judgement run. Seven hours you must wait in this tomb. You will dream your own dreams. You will dance in delirium. You will die and be reborn." His voice was deep and resonant. He spoke down to me because I was a child. I smiled because he sounded lke Uncle Mack on Children's Radio.

"Before the balance trips, any movement will stop the sand and you will not receive the key. You must sit like a statue until the appointed hour, otherwise you will never reach the journey's end."

He saluted me with his staff and left the room.

As the doors closed, the light level dimmed to nothing. The world was black. After a while, my sense of time changed gear and my faculties seemed to drill into the darkness. I noticed, or thought I noticed, a series of odd, little things — noises, dots of light and touches on my skin. Like leaving the city and flopping in a field, a new level of awareness came to me. When all is still, any movement is obvious, the slightest sound stands out, and the least glimmer is like a dawn. Gradually — oh so very, very gradually — the glints, whispers and tremors came toward each other, joined and grew. It or I moved closer. The images became clearer, more distinct, as if I were a moth swooping through the night to a far off flame. The radiancy shaped itself into a ball of light inside which magic figures posed in frozen tableaux.

First of all, I saw naked lovers locked in passion, their skin, shining with sensuous oils. Second was a baby's birth, its skin being cleansed, oiled, and wrapped in linen sheets. Third was the play of children with balm on sores. Fourth was the games of athletes with salve being rubbed into their muscles. Fifth was slaves chained to debt and brutal toil, who were healing their hurts with demulcent creams. Sixth was sickness and old age with liniments used to soothe the joints and limbs. Seventh was the curling up for death with unctions that smelled of the cradle and swaddling being used as a shroud.

A ring of veiled shapes glided through the scenes like ghosts. Among them capered monkey and at each tableau, it picked up a small object. It put them all on a tray and proffered them for my selection. There was a reed-pipe, a rattle, a cymbal, a ram's horn, a bell, a lyre, and a sistrum. A man danced. I grabbed the monkey's arm, tipped everything on to the floor, and took the tray itself. I saw that it was a shallow, round drum. Holding it in one hand, I tapped it with the fingers of my other. The pan of the balance tipped with a resounding boom, the sand stopped, and the bird-man returned and lifted his wand. The walls lifted like stage scenery, the chamber opened like a box, and I was standing before an audience of involved faces.

The Mystic Words

"He has chosen," chanted the bird-man.

The people moaned, "Ah-ay!"

"Not the melody," he intoned, "nor yet the music. He has found out the measure behind all things. He has taken the drum of the first thunder."

They moaned again, "Ah-ay," and all swayed in unison.

"I ask the first question." He turned to face me. "What do you know?"

"The answer that can never be spoken," I replied. No one had schooled me beforehand. In fact, my responses shocked me so much that I gave them in a sort of half-strangled voice.

"I ask the second question," he went on. "What would you know?"

"The cry of a newborn babe who dies in orgasm."

"I ask the third question. What do you need to know?"
"How to calm that cry."

My drum was taken from me by hands of midnight black. A woman stood before me, her body like soot. She danced slowly. Her eyes were stars, her smile a crescent moon. Music filled the air and as she swayed, so her skin changed colour, becoming pale. As she moved to the secret rhythm, her shape changed too, the breasts shrinking, the shoulders spreading, and the wide hips going very slender. Woman changed into man, ebony skin whitened to ivory, and dark hair bleached into blonde locks. And as he pranced with the same abandon, I saw her still, mirrored in the pupils of his sky-blue eyes, smiling and beckoning to me.

Now I yelled but not in terror or ecstasy. It was the wide-open howl of a soul that soars across the firmament like a meteor spewing stars. I was entwined with the aurora borealis and my limbs coiled like rainbows into Celtic knots. Night and day knelt one before the other. The dawn embraced the darkness, and then the enticing arms of dusk slid round the sleepy day. I heard the sighs of Osiris as his bandages were unwound. I heard the swish of falcon's wings as they sailed over seas of tears. "I am black but beautiful," the wisest king[3] sang of her.

I rode a plough drawn by a million toads as we went like a shuttle along the furrows of time. I grubbed out weed, I dibbled in seed, and I beheld the seasons turn from green to gold, and then from red to black. The world was a beach-ball bobbing out to sea. "This is not a game," grumbles the mother. "But we are still winning," answers dad. And he turned toward me and winks.

Aleister winked with an idiot grin and the final phase began.

The Climax

Crowley attacked the ritual with the full volume of his magic voice, firing off salvoes of blazing words in a majestic cannonade. Like a soloist I had seen in Handel's 'Messiah' one Christmas, it was both a religious event and very much a piece of theatre. He was having a whale of a time! Toward the end though, one could hear the asthma starting. It began like a whisper in the tree branches, or a suspicion of smoke on the forest air. Suddenly it was very

---

3. *Song of Solomon*, 1, 5.

serious, with brittle cracking noises that alarmed us all, and him slumped in a chair, gasping and wheezing like a very old man indeed. To this very day, I don't know what impulse moved me. But I leaned over and said "Edward, Edward", in a strangely peaceful voice, for this was his true, given name. I planted my hands on both his shoulders and then said: "You are not an uncaring man." Very slowly, his expression changed from that of a wretch at death's door to that of a pilgrim who has just glimpsed Jerusalem. He held my hands and his breathing came back to normal.

As you may gather, it is all very much a confused welter of memories. Certain things stand out more than others, and these have done good service as signposts in my life. A lot of other things are too ravelled, not so much vague as tangled, and somewhat soggy with emotional gravy. One moment stands out more than anything else though. It was when they opened a curtain and the male 'half' of my dream dancer stood before me. Several faces flashed through my mind, film heroes from Saturday matinees with names like Flash Gordon, Buck Rogers, and the Lone Ranger. Who could have seen inside my soul in order to shape this perfect play-mate?

"Behold your spirit brother," said my father, "your angelic twin and guide." It was a ghost then? A being not of this world? It didn't matter. I was not afraid. When 'he' embraced me a weird warmth ran through me — like the time I drank the whiskey my grandma kept for her medicinal purposes.

"And these", he continued, "are your guards." They were the exact opposite, what with the terrible noises, the awful smell, the howling rage and demented snarls. "They are called," said my father, "the devourers of souls. They will watch your eyes. If they see real anger or true hurt, then they will attack. Nobody will be able to stop them."

Handy, I thought, if I ever got sent to war!

I realize how valuable it would be if I could describe the whole of these events in minute, clinical detail. I've been quizzed often enough, God knows, and even hypnosis has been tried. But I've told you more or less everything that registered on my thirteen year old mind, which had its own criteria and priorities. I was dazzled by different things, and my eyes were drawn by what many would classify as mere oddities and trivia. I did not know how important it was. It never crossed my mind to take notes for some book in the far off future. It is easy to be sceptical about all this. But it would be even easier for me to garnish my memories with a touch of poetic licence! Would that be better, do you suppose, to give the fans something more substantial to chew on by dotting the i's and crossing the t's? In any case, the symbolic levels of meaning are explained in AC's letters to Cara Soror which he began writing in 1943 and which were eventually published by Karl Germer under the title 'Magick without Tears', in 1954. Germer was a wealthy member of the Ordo Templi Orientis in Germany, and he gave Crowley some financial help during some of the times when he was badly-off.

He brought me a present to my bedroom the next morning: an early machine for typing letters which looked very old. Instead of a keyboard, you pointed a hinged needle over a plate of letters and pressed a lever to obtain an imprint on the page of paper. But I was so halting the line of letters rose and fell like a back road in Bolivia. This did not stop me using it for school homework.

"Your script was bad enough," the teacher wrote in red, "but this machine is wholly diabolic!"

If only he'd known where it came from...

24
DJEHUTI

The Lord of Holy Words, three times great, the divider of time. The Magician

A Summing Up

So now, we came to the end of my book. I cannot tell if you have stuck to your old opinions, or whether you've changed them slightly, in the light of what I have said. But whether I have mounted a convincing case or not, I hope you've been interested at the very least.

I liked my father. Half the world tells me I shouldn't have. But why not? He never harmed me. He did nothing wrong that would cause resentment. I have to admit that I was quite fond of the man. No, of course not, fondness is not the same as love, but he wasn't looking for that. As for me, I don't think I was looking for anything in particular at the outset. No, it wasn't love we felt — it was more like warmth between partners who have done it well — Laurel and Hardy for example — or Professor Higgins and Eliza Dolittle.

So there is no hero-worship. I am not blind to faults. And, of course, there were faults a-plenty, but no more and no less than any other human being. They weren't worse as far as he was concerned, they were just more obvious. Even so, it is puzzling why writers dwell on the faults, almost to the exclusion of everything else. During all of his seventy-two years, did the man do no good at all? Was the bad so very, very bad that it merits the treatment it receives? I cannot tell if you, the reader are unbiased. You may feel that I have done the opposite and spoken only of the other side of Crowley. Well, be fair: there was no need for me to re-dig the old ground, was there? The sewage has been sifted by so many experts on that sort of thing, I thought it was best left alone for once.

I have tried to tell you the things that they do not say. They may not even know about them, of course — in which case, I am merely balancing the account. There's no denying that it has been a very long time — forty-six years since I last saw him! That is one hell of a distance for the mind's telescope to peer, so I'm not going to brag that I have included everything, much less claim that I have got it all exactly right. But you can understand that, can't you? I've grown rusty, dusty and rheumatic! There's a certain stiffness in the fine-focus adjustment ring. It's not important what I've forgotten — but have I remembered enough?

Before anyone suggests it, and they will, I promise that I have not padded things out with my own invention. It was a sore temptation at times. Luckily, one idea led on to another and bit by bit the memories came back and fell into place. Each re-write, each revision, I sort of cleared away more weeds and found 'lost' thoughts. Besides, where would it have got us if I'd tried to make it up? Crowley would not have liked it! Magick was not something he lied about. So I must risk irking the critics; that's better than perturbing the old man's spirit.

I'm not a professional writer with lots of experience in this sort of thing. You can tell that much from reading my book, I'm sure. But then again, my subject did have flaws.

Three Flaws

From my stand-point, Aleister Crowley was dogged by three great defects in his personality. I'm in a good position to talk about these remember — I am his son and a psychologist.

1. Despite a good education and useful connections, he was socially inept. He was gauche, naive, clumsy and quite unable to see another person's point of view. In terms of magic, yes, he was a great leader, none better in fact. But in terms of daily life, he was as stubborn as a mule, bitter in his grudges, and so thoughtless with many of his own followers that he simply alienated them. When former friends have not remembered him with appropriate kindness, one can't altogether blame them. We must not judge them too harshly because, all things considered, Aleister Crowley was not an easy man to get on with. There were compensations, of course. He was a powerful magician when all's said and done. But those who knew him personally, acted the way they did because he was damnably difficult. Perhaps he made a lot of effort for me, but I don't think he did for anyone else.

2. He said himself that his childhood was not a happy one. But it wasn't all that miserable either. The family were wealthy enough. There was no physical cruelty or neglect, and no planned campaign of emotional or mental torture. Aleister Crowley was not deprived. Other children have been born into strict, Christian families but have not spent their lives anguishing about it. The way he himself describes things, we could have expected much deeper scars and much greater problems. I have a strong suspicion that he exaggerated the facts.

Despite the things he said, Crowley loved his mother, but he never believed that she loved him, and this is the most telling point. Many of his words and actions can be seen as misplaced revenge. True, most children have conflicts with their parents, and all pass through a stage of natural rebelliousness. In the Crowley household, this was not allowed. There were no outlets, no pranks and no high spirits. This is why he was so often moved by the spirit of mischief. He loved being a clown, dressing-up, and dropping banana skins. He was looking for something he could brandish in his parents' faces just to prove that they were wrong and they had failed. To this extent at least, he never grew up and so a large percentage of the 'evil' was just him going too far. There was a side of him that couldn't be restrained. He was still a rumbustious child.

3. If he lacked insight, he wasn't much better with foresight either. He might have been telepathic, clairvoyant and the other wonderful things — but he simply did not appreciate where his clumsy dealings with the press would lead. This is not to say there was no hypocrisy in Fleet Street. Of course there was. The magazine John Bull certainly had it in for him! The owner of the publication, Horatio Bottomley, whilst reviling Crowley was playing around with fraudulent stock at the same time, and cheating the public on a grand scale.

But Crowley did nothing to help matters. You might even say he was his own worst enemy. He didn't see the danger. He never imagined he'd lose. He always said that any publicity was better than being unknown. Of course, he was astute enough to realize that behind Lord Northcliffe, Lord Rothermere and the other press-barons, there was a much larger power: the Freemasons. He knew what he was dealing with — he just didn't deal with it very well!

When we tot up the score and look at the final result, a fair judgement would be: Aleister Crowley was not a wicked man. Or, as his beloved King Lear put it, "I am a man more sinned against than sinning." In my personal opinion, this was true.

The Ungodly?
Colin Wilson[1] says "Sex is certainly the key to Crowley's mentality..." He uses sturdier words still, a little later on. "Crowley's over-reaction to authority was compounded with an equally unrealistic over-reaction to sex, which led him to believe he was being iconoclastic when he was only sticking his tongue out at long-dead Victorians."

Up to now, I have always admired Mr Wilson's work. I remember winning a debate with a famous professor of philosophy about the merits of his first book, 'The Outsider'. Like countless other people, I considered it to be an outstanding piece of work. Since then, though, I have found Mr. Wilson dazzling us more with his sheer breadth of knowledge, so that the average reader may not notice its frequent lack of depth.

In this book about Crowley, for example, a slight sprinkling of academic modesty would not have gone amiss amidst all his strong assertions. I am referring here to those important signals that separate the *facts* we are citing from the *construction* we want to thrust on them. Hearsay, for instance, carries less weight with sober judges than it does with shoppers in Oxford Street. Of course, his book was not intended as evidence to be produced in court, but at the same time — there was a man's reputation on trial! It is easy to tell when an author is being impartial, and when he is pushing for a verdict. For example, he ought not to suppose that his personal conviction is evidence. There are terms he could use — 'in my opinion' for example, or even 'I think'. Far too often though Mr. Wilson simply says 'It is'! I have tried to apply my own advice in this book. I have an advantage over Mr Wilson though — I am writing of someone I knew and not just someone I have read about. Why oh why are strangers so dogmatic? Our subject, let me remind you, is a man and his life. Yes, he is dead now and from a legal point of view there is nothing to stop an author from probing all aspects of his subject and analyzing what he finds.

1. Wilson, C. *Aleister Crowley, The Nature of the Beast,* Aquarian Press, 1987.

Within certain bounds, we have a perfect right to be curious, to ask questions and to search for answers.

But by dying, we should not imagine that a human being has been down-graded to just a corpse. A man, even when dead, is something more than an object on a laboratory table. Even pathologists, when doing an autopsy on a criminal, try to be clinical, detached and show some respect for the cadaver. Even an undertaker leaves the deceased some dignity. But Mr. Wilson treats Crowley as fair game and ignores the fact that this was once a man, who had existence, who walked, talked, felt, dreamed, suffered and was occasionally disappointed by people. He was created by the very same powers that later went on to create Mr. Wilson and even if he were as vile and obnoxious as Mr. Wilson suggests, he was many other things too.

Alas, when Mr. Wilson has finished with Crowley, it is not so much a case he has made out so much as a bucket he has filled.

How much I wish that Crowley could read what Mr. Wilson has written! I can picture his reaction exactly. He would wonder what on earth he had done to this person. Then he would fix him with a steely gaze, like sticking a beetle to cork. "Mr. Wilson," he'd say. "There is a saying that he who dies pays all debts!" His voice would be freezing, flat and full of meaning. Mr. Wilson would not be sure if he'd just been rebuked, or promised a trip to the world beyond.

Quick-Change

If Mr Wilson meant to write a biography, he fails on two counts. One: he doesn't approach his subject from all angles but selects the ones that help his case and neglects the ones that would have been awkward. Two: he accepts *a priori* that Crowley is guilty as charged and uses his skill to show why that judgement should stand. I consider the judgement is wrong. I would like to call the court's attention to more significant matters. Of course, I am not a biographer by trade. I am only writing my own memories.

Very few people knew Crowley as closely or as long as I did. Is this why I am alone in recognising that he was a walking theatrical hamper? He could pull out cloaks, masks and make-up at will. So what makes the others think they knew the real Crowley? I saw him before as well as during meetings, so I know how he rang the subtle changes. I saw the show so often I could have played it for him, if only I'd been the right size! He had characters galore and used a different one for each person who approached him. None of them was wholly different. They had a great deal in common, in fact. Shall we say: more like variations on a theme than totally separate inventions.

Among a group or at a party, you might have thought that someone would notice. Not at all. He just drew the broad features broader and left out more and more detail. Hence, everyone felt that here was the Aleister they had always known. All of which was quite deliberate, you understand. In the field of mental medicine, it is not too rare for a psychotic patient to be able to withdraw into any one of several other identities. Crowley was not the least bit mad, but he could have broken the record!

I knew him in the Green Room, so to speak. I watched him conjure with these images and try out new ones. On two occasions only I caught him unawares, and he panicked like the Phantom of the Opera caught without his mask! I accepted all this. I took him for what he seemed and it was a long time after that I started to form any private opinions. But that's how it is with family: you simply react. It is easy now, with the benefit of hindsight, to say that Crowley didn't wish to be known. But I think that's true. Instead of anyone seeing him 'whole', he handed each one a piece from a broken mirror.

It isn't uncommon, this reluctance to expose one's inner self. About half of us enjoy doing psychological tests but the other half refuses nervously. In one hospital, a young man suffering from only a minor condition went berserk when he saw a pretty nurse reading his medical notes! He fancied her. But she had seen inside his secret cupboard. He went violently mad.

Where does this lead us? Well, I don't think Crowley understood himself. He was the mystery that he spent so much of his life trying to solve. This is where his system of magic does triumph because it can be a pathway to insight and self-awareness. It is the same goal that inspires a thousand other paths and it was this pilgrimage of the soul, or sacred quest, which first drew him to magic. Is it not so for all of us? When the unknown catches our eye, is it not the authentic inner self which feels that it has recognized a lifebelt?

We have all felt something pluck at our sleeve — the same kind of vague urgency that calls swallows to come North in spring. We too need to go elsewhere and to be something other. We too search for a reality behind this one.

Drugs

Crowley and drugs — that is harder to deal with. For me there was no problem: I didn't see any drugs and even if I had, I would have called it a sickness I think. Personally I have no time for drugs. I loathe them because of the damage they do and I condemn them spiritually because they undermine the rule of the will. In Crowley's case though I sincerely believe the basic cause was his asthma. As he got older, he also felt very let-down by his friends. "My band of knock-kneed knights," he called them bitterly. "Fair-weather friends who quit at the first flake of snow in my eyes."

He had the habit of saying things like that — things which sounded as if they were well-known quotations. It amused him no end to watch people racking their brains and trying to find the source. He made most of them up on the spur of the moment, simply to confuse people. They cottoned on to his trick only if they began to notice the twinkle in his eyes. He wasn't always on top of the world. Far from it. He could be quite sad too. This wasn't morbid depression though. Neither was it the generalized kind of pessimistic outlook one sometimes finds in old age. No, he would sometimes sigh rather more than he smiled, as if he had noticed the grey clouds creeping up on the horizon. Even in his most boisterous moods, his laughter seemed tinged with regret. I had the impression, I put it no stronger, that he was wistful about some personal inability to love.

As I write the words, I know for certain he would have objected to them and, indeed, I have to admit the possibility that I'm wrong. I don't think so however. Aleister Crowley didn't much care for anyone in particular. This wasn't egoism; nothing as simple as that. He had been very active sexually — according to some authors, not even stopping for sleep — but he was never able to feel any deep, lasting love. This great, universal passion had not been the lynchpin of his life and — he was mystified by the fact.

On the other hand, he very much liked being loved. When I brought him a small present and put on a ticket "With love", there would be tears in his eyes as he opened it. Just like any other child,

I learned quickly that the best method to wheedle my way round any objections he had was to make a big show of hugs and soppy words. He adored it. Even when he was in high dudgeon and fulminating against the world, an arm through his arm and a sympathetic pat on the hand worked wonders. If you hurt him, forgiveness came most easily if you showed real concern. It was better than any apology.

25
OURSIR

Lord of nature and god of the dead

An Overstated Case

He did have enemies, of course. I don't mean rivals, competitors or people who envied his flare. I mean implacable and deadly enemies. Most of these were direct opponents who believed he represented a danger to everything they believed in. Since what they believed in was rather unwholesome, I take this as a strong point in his favour.

Another point is this: it is hardly imaginable that anyone could ever have been as wicked as Crowley has been depicted! It is simply not credible that what he did was so inflammatory that people are still out to get him, forty odd years after his death! Come to that, if it was indeed my father's conduct that they hated, why should they now have turned on me? And — oh yes — before you say it: I have been psycho-analysed and tested for paranoia! It is one of the standard procedures when you choose to study psychology because they want to be sure that your motivations are not morbid.

They have a saying in the North of England: "if the devil doesn't much like you, then you can't be all bad!" Don't you think in Crowley's case, his enemies have overdone it somewhat? It reminds one of the verdict of the Witch-finder General: "... not only did she consort with the devil and commit unnatural acts, but when she broke wind mice and worms came out of her fundament, when she was stretched on the rack she did utter wicked oaths against our Lord Protector, and when she was ducked in the village pond she said that all bystanders would rot in hell. She did smell might high also." When the accusations include everything but the kitchen sink, don't you begin to smell a rat?

There is very strong evidence to show that Crowley was the victim of a hate-campaign. I don't want to brow-beat you, but I would beg the jury to think things over calmly. I write only those things I know about. I quote Crowley's own words whenever I can. I haven't got any axe to grind, and it would gain me nothing if Crowley's name were cleared and he was canonized. So I put it to you straight: is it not remarkable that no other magician or occultist is ever attacked at a personal level? I ask you in all candour: is there nothing spicy about Madame Blavatsky's private life? Were there no rumours about Eliphas Levi and little boys? What do you know of the sexual depravities of John Dee, Paracelsus, Papus, Dion Fortune, Gurdjieff, Rudolf Steiner or even Adolf Hitler? Were all other occultists doctored at birth? Did none of them ever do anything discreditable? Were they perfect and only Crowley a man? No, of course not. But people write about their magic because their magical theories did not rock the boat!

To be sure, there were one or two odd-balls among them but, apart from being magicians, they were all decent enough chaps. Crowley on the other hand... he let the side down. Talked in class. Smoked behind the loos. He did not do what he was supposed to do. He refused to conform!

The Importance of his Magick
Or to put it another way: his magic was getting somewhere so they refuse to talk about it, and they do their best to discredit the man. Messages were sent out hither and thither across Europe, and not just by telegraph, telephone or the Royal Mail — but also in the diplomatic bag. How many times was he expelled from this or that country? How many times were his lectures cancelled by the authorities? We are talking about an era in which Archdukes were being assassinated, when thousands were slaughtered at Gallipoli, when influenza was an epidemic killer, when Wall Street crashed and the great depression hit the world economy. The King of England quit the throne to marry a divorcee! Yet newspapers and governments found time to keep an eye on Aleister Crowley! That, as my son once told me, is weird, mad!

Attempts had been made on his life. They were not carried out in any obvious way and he very much doubted if the police would take any trouble to investigate. So he said nothing. There was no point. Either they'd have laughed and called it paranoia or they'd have accused him of seeking more publicity. In any case, the methodology they used was occult. To have used open violence might have aroused public interest.

Throughout his long life, and ever since his death, there has been one, long attempt to destroy the man's character[1] There has been no let up since the days he quarrelled with the Golden Dawn and pocketed certain documents. It got much worse after the affair with Rudolf Hess. If you like, it is a kind of war.

The accidents, obstructions, trip-ups and pratfalls: they were not pure chance. The cards were stacked. The horse was nobbled. They moved the pieces behind his back. Evidently, it was all done by someone with the power to do it, which narrows down the field a lot. The Hermetic Order of the Golden Dawn, the Ordo Templi Orientis, The Rosicrucians and the Illuminati — all had links with, or were divisions of, Freemasonry. They are rather a tight family, the Freemasons — one for all and all for one. The point being that you do not join, you wait until you are invited. The riff-raff and hoi polloi are not invited. Wherever they form a lodge, their power-base is built among the worthies of the social structure: bankers, publishers, the law, the church, Whitehall, the army and influential members of the Jewish community. They had a meeting to discuss the Crowley business. Delegates came from England, France, Germany, and Switzerland but not (possibly because they were black) from America! They put their heads together and they have been colluding ever since.

At the beginning, I was naive enough to imagine that Crowley himself was paid to send a trickle of scandal in the direction of Fleet Street. "Nothing I do now will interest them very much," he said to me. "Not as pretty as I used to be. One more blast perhaps — to pay for my funeral. After that, mark my words: it will not stop!" I didn't see what he was getting at. I missed the point. You must work it out for yourselves.

An Awkward Customer

He was anti the government. He was against the establishment. He derided the status quo. He couldn't yet see how things might be changed but he was more than acquainted with the mysterious

---

1. cf Howard, M. *The Occult Conspiracy,* Rider 1989.

anarchist who figured in the famous 'Siege of Sydney Street'. This created great headlines at the time and is always quoted as one of the milestones marking Winston Churchill's career — he was the Home Secretary at the time. The man's code-name was Peter the Painter; but that's not what Aleister called him. He had a certain sympathy for the man's aims, but never got really fired by politics. He called that "using the enemy's favourite weapon".

In any case, with the Second World War looming, he didn't see any agitators being able to change events. The government was pouring vast sums of money into boosting the patriotic spirit. Millions were going to die. The nation had to be got ready for the coming casualty figures. No, Aleister did not speak out against the social structure though he heartily disapproved of it. He would have been attacked mercilessly.

Crowley was one hundred per cent in favour of Liberty, Equality and Fraternity. In his opinion though, the French had botched the job and opened the way to decadence and corruption.

"The French are taught at school, and it's the one thing they never forget, that they are right and everyone else is wrong. If ever the slightest doubt is expressed, they will prove the matter by tearing up the cobble-stones and raising barricades. Believe me, once across the channel it is every man for himself... even more so for the woman!"

He chuckled rather naughtily. "It's no coincidence you know, that the French national symbol is a cock!"

Despite the lurid mythology, Crowley dominated no one and neither did he seek to do so. He was incapable of managing his private finances, let alone running an Occult Order or a Secret Society. As a young Trade Unionist said of his own president: "he couldn't organize a piss-up in a brewery!" In the managerial sense, Crowley was totally inept. He has the reputation for being able to dominate, like the hypnotist villain in the novel 'Trilby', by using the sheer power of his will.

Well, no matter what people say, and no matter what they are reported to have said, the fact is that not one victim has been produced. Rumours abound but nothing concrete has ever been brought forward. In short, people thought of Crowley in a certain way and so they described him in that certain way.

Master of Evil?

Colin Wilson repeats a story told by John Symonds' wife who seems to have got a powerful sense of evil. "Yes, evil haunted that face, but the years had diluted its strength." They were talking about Crowley's trek across China, apparently. Nevertheless, her antennae were finely tuned. She felt that "... the room had become small and oppressive, and he flooded me again with a sense of evil, so that I visibly shivered." Very colourful indeed but, pardon my indelicacy, a lady's private impressions, even well-honed by years of repetition, are far from solid or reliable evidence. They can tell us just as much about her state of mind as they do about Crowley.

Mr. Wilson also states "... it was this 'criminal' element in him (Crowley) that was sensed by people who felt he was evil. It is interesting to note Crowley's habit of relieving his bowels on people's carpets... a frequent feature of burglaries... a gesture of rebellion." Mr. Wilson is straining this analogy too far, I fear. On the one hand, the 'criminal' element has not been established. On the other, Crowley did not have a 'habit' of defecating on carpets. As for Mr. Wilson's interpretation of the act, there are alternatives. Does he know, for instance, that psychiatrists often receive a gift of turds? The gesture is made by a patient who has regressed to an infantile mental state. Remembering how pleased mummy was when he used the toilet correctly, he tries to win a smile from his doctor or gain a little love. The turd is often wrapped or put in a gift-box. But once a bond of trust is formed, they slap it, still warm, straight in your hand.

To set the record straight, Crowley once called on a wealthy friend, hoping to cadge a loan. He sent up his visiting card, but the butler brought back the message that his master was "not at home at this time". Crowley was so humiliated, he dropped his slacks and left his answer on the carpet. The butler must have felt professional envy for his coolness. "Tell him it was the Great Dane," snapped Crowley, quitting the scene. The butler quietly cleared things up but, instead of resigning, he sold the story to a newspaper. Alas, he did not think to take a photograph so we have only his word for it.

26
KHENSU

*A moon-god who can incarnate his own double,
his name means the navigator*

Crowley's Appearance
"Crowley wanted to be a magician because he wanted power," asserts Wilson, "power over other people." In support of which he points to a resemblance to Adolf Hitler. This was first noted, he adds by one of Crowley's female admirers. If this is why she admired him it tells us much about her eye-sight! Mr. W. Somerset Maugham wrote a novel called 'The Magician'. The main character, Oliver Haddo, is based on Aleister Crowley. This is his description: "... a man of great size, two or three inches more than six feet high; but the most imposing thing about him was a vast obesity. His paunch was of imposing dimensions. His face was large and fleshy..."

I confess that I never met Hitler, but like everyone else I did see photographs and films. This thumb-nail sketch is not at all like him. Oliver Hardy or Edward VII — possibly. But not Hitler. But had the female admirer been relying on hearsay too? It is risky, relying on other people's impressions.

Or has this something to do with the Jungian technique of "active imagination", to which Mr. Wilson also refers?

Gurdjieff
One evening, Aleister was talking about Zen Buddhism, and he touched on the art of the Japanese Haiku. This is a form of poem in which two complimentary parts are expressed in only three lines of seventeen syllables. When you try it in English, you need to relax the rules a bit. This is the one he offered me:

"Policemen work for the law but believe they are the law. A man who was queer got arrested for asking the time!" He was having a bit of fun, of course. "If you want to know the time, ask a policeman," he explained, by quoting an old, music-hall song. "But Nancy-boys accost men by asking for the time, or a light. Do you get it?"

"Yes," I nodded. "I give it three out of ten."

It wasn't very brilliant really, just puzzling and amusing. But he was right about people exaggerating their own importance. They do tend to become that which they were meant merely to represent. A butler is one example. A man who sells railway tickets is another. But we are not here to judge Crowley as a stand-up comic. He was often baulked by the incapacity of human language to express his ideas. He warned me against taking them too literally. The 'Crowning of the will', for example, does not mean 'being governed by the will' or 'letting will rule'. He was saying that emotions ought to be kept to one side whenever possible because they tie us down.

Buddha would have agreed.

Gurdjieff would not have disagreed.

Mr. Wilson refers to Gurdjieff quite a lot and speaks very favourably indeed of this teacher from Russia. He says he was a magician who knew about the strange powers of the will "... although he never used them as Crowley did, purely for his own satisfaction." He refers also to Gurdjieff's amazing ability a. to converse by telepathy, b. to cause girls to faint by playing the piano, and c. to exercise a direct sexual influence on women. Not all that different from Crowley, I would have thought.

"Gurdjieff and Crowley seem to have met only once," he goes on, "when Crowley went to tea at Gurdjieff's priory at Fontainbleau; Gurdjieff apparently kept a watchful eye on Crowley, and C. S. Nott said of this meeting: 'I got a strong *impression* (my emphasis) of two magicians, the white and the black — the one strong, powerful, full of light: the other also powerful, but heavy, dull, ignorant'."

He sounds like a cat who is lapping up cream. Is it not unusual though, for a White magician to invite a Black magician for tea and scones? The idea is as absurd as the Pope handing out Garibaldi biscuits to the Mafia! And this C.S. Nott who had such strong impressions — did he know why the two men were meeting? Did he whole-heartedly approve? I suspect his nose was put out of joint, his optic nerve too, because he already hated Crowley and already idolized Gurdjieff.

Not to put too fine a point on it: Mr. Nott was one of Gurdjieff's followers. I am given to understand[1] that Mr. Wilson is too. Now I'm not a lawyer. All I know on the subject is what I gleaned from 'A Fish Named Wanda'. But if he had told us this, it would have helped us to weigh his words more carefully.

I can't say if Mr. Nott or Mr. Wilson knew it, but Gurdjieff and Crowley were rivals. However, they were not enemies. There was no feud between them and neither ever said a bad word about the other. As a matter of fact, they were on the same side. Like Field Marshall Montgomery and General Patton, they were quite agreed on the final objectives but they differed about the best strategy. Freud, Jung and Adler were the founding fathers of modern psychiatry, you might say, but they went their separate ways because they disagreed on emphasis. Crowley and Gurdjieff were much closer than that!

Curious Parallels

The air can be cleared quite quickly if we review a few facts which are not disputed by anyone:

1: Gurdjieff was born in 1877 and died in 1949, aged 72. 2: Crowley was born in 1875 and died in 1947, aged 72. 3: Gurdjieff visited Tibet and the Middle East. 4: Crowley went to China and the Middle East. 5: No one can explain the source of Gurdjieff's doctrine. 6: No one can explain the source of Crowley's doctrine. 7: Both men met Rasputin near to Mount Athos. 8: Rasputin was a member of the Khlysty Sect. 9: There are striking parallels between the teachings of all three men.

Yes, I can see how irritating it must be when I give clues without providing the actual answer. But I'm not yet free to say all that I know. However there is one fact I can confirm. It is common knowledge that Gurdjieff managed to vanish from Paris at the outset of the war and that he did not make his reappearance until 1946. In other words, there was a seven year absence that no one has been able to explain so far. Rumour says that one or two of his French followers may have known his whereabouts.

Yes, they did indeed. One was the gentleman who owned the

---

1. Butterworth, J. *Cults and New Faiths,* Lion Publishing 1981, p. 16.

chateau near Boulogne. I mentioned it earlier in the book, if you remember, as the place where I was conceived. A second was an officer belonging to the French Secret Service. He and a few others had had their heads together with my father at the time when they were supposed to be expelling him from France! I mentioned that earlier too. It all took place in a small flat, a stone's throw away from the Elysée Palace, of all places. The third was something to do with publishing and later on in the war he became a prominent figure in the French Resistance.

There may well have been others, but somehow I doubt it. I think the idea was to keep the business under wraps. In any case, these three gentlemen accompanied Gurdjieff on an ordinary trip to England. They landed at Dover in late August, 1939, just a few days before England declared war on Germany.

The three gentlemen brought Gurdjieff to meet my father. I wasn't present on that occasion although he had told me that something was happening. I was introduced to him some two days later at breakfast. I remember him saying how well the English ate. I went on meeting Mr. Gurdjieff off and on throughout the duration of the war. He did not lodge with my father, who never stayed at one address very long. But he passed the seven years at the same boarding house in Frinton which was the "nicer part" of Clacton-on-Sea in those days.

Unknown Teachings
It is right to end with a few examples of Crowley's hidden teaching. These are the ideas he gave to personal students and never put in any book. It wasn't secret in the sense of withheld or guarded. He just felt that some things can only be taught by word of mouth, the Master face to face with his apprentices. The calumnies have gone on long enough. It is time these things were known.

I can't say everything. We worked together for seven years! Out of all that he told me, I've selected a few things that seem typical. I have not edited them. I have left nothing out, nor have I softened the language. This is the Aleister Crowely that *I* knew, and he was not the man described in other books.

Everyone must have heard that story about his 'elixir of life pills'. If you remember, he sold them at something like twenty-five guineas a box, and there were plenty of discerning customers.

Now, all they contained was chalk, sugar and a dribble or two of semen! Nevertheless, the clients were very well pleased with results and not one of them complained.

"Yes," he told me, "a great success, my boy. Isn't magic amazing?" He laughed uproariously and slapped the table in mirth. "They all think how horrible, how disgusting, how indecent! But still they can't explain why the bloody things were so powerful."

There was still a smile on his face but he became much calmer. "I'll let you into a secret, my lad," he leaned over and whispered in a conspiratorial way. "In actual fact, it wasn't my own sperm! The Crowley yield was being used for other purposes, elsewhere!"

The sceptic will persist in the placebo theory — the notion that even useless substances will work if someone believes in their effectiveness. In other words, they are saying the pills had no intrinsic curative value at all. It was all in the customer's mind. Well, this was the first placebo drug to be one hundred per cent successful.

The only other explanation is that the sperm did have some magical effect. There wasn't a lot of it, mind. One single ejaculate in hundreds of pills. We are talking of infinitesimal proportions. Evidently, there was some unknown chap knocking about London, blessed with a set of homeopathic testicles which would have made him, and Crowley, rich. Aleister was so delighted with the sudden injection of ready cash, he must of thought about it. The strange thing was — he respected the source of the sperm. More than that, he seemed to be awed.

He spoke of the beauty in Nature which was super-natural. It existed in both worlds, *here* as well as *there*. He didn't mean the nature walks at a primary school. It had nothing to do with pretty flowers or fluffy-tailed rabbits. He never spoke in the cliches of travel films because his view was not a romantic panorama of mountains, clouds, sunset and lakes. He saw things the way Red Indians do, as if this were home. "If you wish to hear the spirits," he said, "go and sleep in the clover."

On the eve of a ritual he said: "Terror, nervousness, and mystic pride bring greater triumph than doing daring things by the bicycle shed. Very few schoolboys can stop a storm." Or again, while waiting for someone in desperate need: "Each orgasm is an encounter with death. Search for the courage that makes you unafraid of living. If reason is impossible, confront their minds with forbidden fears and concepts that seem unbearable. A person's violence is rooted in the putrid filth of dead emotions."

The nicest was when he said: "What is the Master's work? He turns violets into roses. He trains them to have stout stems. He tells them to guard their souls with rings of thorns to ward off the nuzzling beasts. Then he teaches them that their own perfume can bring hither the power that will change the world."

But lastly, ultimately, the most splendid of all: "Every man and woman is a star. Some fall. Some burst into dust. Some shine on steadily through the long, dark night. We start them off, we Masters, by handing them a candle."